P9-DZY-031

Courtyard Gardens

635.9671 Mus

Musgrave, T.
Courtyard gardens.

PRICE: $17.33 (3710/an/st)

Courtyard Gardens

INNISFIL PUBLIC LIBRARY
P.O. BOX 7049
INNISFIL, ON L9S 1A8

Toby Musgrave

HEARST BOOKS New York

For Aulani,
Thank you for bringing so much to my life

Text and courtyard designs copyright
© Toby Musgrave 2000
Illustration, design and layout copyright
© Jacqui Small 2000

This book was previously published as
a hardcover.

All rights reserved. The written instructions
and photographs in this volume are
intended for the personal use of the
reader and may be reproduced for that
purpose only. Any other use, especially
commercial use, is forbidden under law
without the written permission of the
copyright holder.

Publisher **Jacqui Small**
Editorial consultant **Erica Hunningher**
Editor **Casey Horton**
Designer **Maggie Town**
Illustrator **Helen Smythe**
Picture researcher **Emily Hedges**
Courtyard design **Toby Musgrave**
US gardening consultant **Bruce Riggs**
Production **Geoff Barlow**

The Library of Congress has catalogued
the hardcover edition as follows:

Musgrave, Toby.
  Courtyard gardens:
  imaginative ideas for outdoor living /
  by Toby Musgrave.
     p. cm.
  ISBN 1-58816-002-5
  1. Courtyard gardening.
  2. Courtyard gardens. 1. Title.
  SB473.2.M87 2001
  635.9'671—dc21
                              00-039613

10 9 8 7 6 5 4 3 2 1

First Paperback Edition 2005
Published by Hearst Books
A Division of Sterling Publishing Co., Inc.
387 Park Avenue South,
New York, NY 10016

Country Living Gardener is a trademark
owned by Hearst Magazines Property,
Inc., in USA, and Hearst
Communications, Inc., in Canada. Hearst
Books is a trademark owned by Hearst
Communications, Inc.

www.cl-gardener.com

Distributed in Canada by Sterling
Publishing
C/o Canadian Manda Group,
165 Dufferin Street
Toronto, Ontario M6K 3H6
Canada

Printed in China

ISBN 1-58816-456-X

contents

the art
of courtyard gardening

A courtyard provides a place of refuge in which to retreat from the rest of the world. This has always been so, for the courtyard garden is as old as garden making itself. By deciding to create a courtyard garden of your own, you are carrying on an ancient and respected tradition, one that began at least 5,000 years ago.

Ancient Egyptian tomb paintings depict the first courtyard gardens as sanctuaries, open to the sky and enclosed by walls or palisades that gave protection from marauders and the hot desert winds. Within these walls were shady, verdant oases where rectangular pools, fed with water from the Nile, were edged with flowerbeds and shaded by tall trees and vine-clad pergolas—each an island of tranquillity and spiritual refreshment.

Down through the centuries, the style of courtyard design (which, in part, is dependent on the prevailing climate and available plants) has varied from country to country and changed with time. Yet the very popularity of the courtyard garden has ensured that there is now a rich, global legacy of garden making ideas, which can be used to solve modern design dilemmas in all sorts of interesting and intriguing ways.

The tradition of courtyard gardening continues today as the perfect solution for creating an extension to the home. It offers greater scope for outdoor living than simply building a sun porch, and its potential is not limited by its size. As well as providing a place of beauty and restfulness, a room outside is somewhere to entertain and cultivate plants, a corner in which to refresh the mind and revitalize the spirit.

In order to create a courtyard that reflects your lifestyle and personality, and meets your aesthetic needs, time and budget, a well-thought-out design and careful planning are essential. Approached as a sequential set of tasks, this can be an enjoyable and rewarding process, providing you with the opportunity to express your creative spirit at each stage, and a great sense of achievement once the tasks have been completed. Before you do anything, establish precisely what you want and decide on the style of the courtyard. Ask yourself what its purpose is to be, and how you want it to look. It can be formal or informal, designed along historical lines or incorporating elements from different periods and cultures. By looking to the past and adapting a design, making it suitable for a modern lifestyle, you will enjoy the novelty and excitement of bringing history to life and creating a garden that is relevant, affordable, attainable, and a little out of the ordinary.

Study the designs in Style Sources (pages 14-52), which offers ten three-dimensional garden plans complete with detailed descriptions and comprehensive lists of plantings and materials. The plans have been inspired by courtyard garden styles from the past—ancient Rome through Europe and Japan to the Americas—and include a glance into the future. However, you need not restrict yourself to an historical style. Courtyards can be designed to meet a specific theme or purpose—romantic, easy to maintain, a place to entertain guests, and so on. A further eight designs, styled along these lines, can be found in Designing by Theme (pages 56-90).

Having chosen a theme or style, decide on the framework features—those items and materials that establish the shape, layout, and mood. Some of the ever-increasing range of materials and furnishings for the structural elements of the courtyard are

A strong and well planned design (opposite) that utilizes a range of complementary materials is essential in creating an overall feeling of space well used.

The geometric pattern (above right) of box hedging emphasizes the symmetrical pattern of the courtyard, which is edged with brick. This parterre demonstrates how relevant traditional elements can be to the modern courtyard designer. It also illustrates how the design should take into consideration views within the garden.

Enclosure provides privacy (center right), and where it forms part of the garden's framework, it should be attractive. Focal features, such as sculpture, are essential, as they draw the eye to specific points in the garden, while trees cast cool, dappled shade.

Planting softens the hard landscaping (right) and vertical structures, while the mirror in the trellis work shelter provides an optical illusion, which adds an element of surprise.

described in The Framework (pages 94-120). The type of boundary and any internal divisions need to be chosen to match the overall style, as do the plants and paving materials. Decide whether or not you want water and, if so, in what form—tinkling rills for relaxation, a spouting fountain for excitement, or a calm, limpid pool to reflect the sky.

Lighting is another important element to consider, and should be planned from the outset, so that electric outlets can be installed early in the building process. Architectural plants, some of which might already be in situ if you are transforming an existing garden, will add living structure and are also useful for providing a link between the house and the garden.

The features and effects that furnish your courtyard must also be chosen to match the overall style. Sculpture, containers, shading, and furniture heighten the mood, increase interest, and introduce ornamentation. For each garden style there are many different ornamental elements that can be included, all of which are dealt with in Decorative Features and Effects (pages 122-138).

The third stage in creating your garden is to work with a scale drawing of your courtyard, made on tracing paper. If it is to be a completely new garden, then this piece of paper will show little more than the shape of the plot, doors from the house, north-south orientation, and any views beyond the garden that might be exploited by apertures in boundaries. Orientation will reveal sunny and shady areas of the plot, and will influence where you site your sitting area or water feature. Note, too, any slopes that might need to be transformed into a flight of steps, or areas that could be excavated to create a pond. If you are remaking an existing garden, you

Asymmetry and bold architectural forms (right) are the basic elements in this modern courtyard. The design both reflects and contrasts with the landscape beyond, incorporating the natural forms of plant and stone with cast concrete and an artificial watercourse.

Decoratively patterned floor and wall tiles (below) contribute to the elegance of this Islamic-influenced courtyard. This is a low-maintenance garden, perfect for relaxing—as the cat demonstrates so well.

should mark on the plan the position of any plants and features you want to retain.

With the outlines mapped out, play around with a soft pencil and eraser, fitting the new features and ornaments into the space in a unified way. As part of this process, remember that you will be creating views from the house windows.

Resolving the practical aspects will make the garden fall into place. If you have thought about how you will move around the space (paths and steps) and how you will use it, your courtyard will be well proportioned and will feel restful and calm. If you stamp it with your own individuality, you will know when the arrangement looks right.

The final step is to plan the planting. Keep in mind the old adage "right plant, right place," and select plants that will survive in the climate and grow in your soil (the latter requirement can be mitigated by using pots); otherwise you will fight a losing battle. Dig two or three holes to test the depth of the topsoil. If it is less than 12in, you should increase the depth by importing some topsoil. If your soil is heavy clay, you will need to improve it by incorporating organic manure and washed sand, and if you live in an area of high rainfall, consider installing subsoil drainage. Use a soil-testing kit to test the soil pH (less than 7 is acid, 7 is neutral, and above 7 is alkaline) and make a note of the type of plants that are growing well in neighboring gardens.

For a catalog of plants suitable for courtyards, see Plants for Courtyard Gardens (pages 142-155), which provides profiles of more than 400 individual plants, arranged by their use. This will make selecting the right plant for the right place that much easier. However, if you want to be purist when creating an historically influenced design, remember that you should really use only period correct plants—plant species that were available during that particular period of time.

When you have your plan on paper you are ready to build, but it is wise to think the project through and construct a work schedule that breaks the task into stages. Begin with the hard landscaping, such as walls, raised beds, paving, paths, and water features, then move to the ornaments and features and finish with the planting. For certain jobs, you will need professional help, but for the rest, do it yourself. If you make an occasional mistake, think of it as part of the process of arriving at the right solution. When it is complete, you can stand back with pride and know you have created your own piece of paradise— an apt word, derived from the Old Persian, *pairidaeza*, meaning "a walled space."

The Mediterranean-style courtyard (left) relies to a large extent on the use of container plants and hard surfaces. Here dark green foliage provides a rich contrast to deep pink walls.

Architectural plants (below) can be positioned to draw attention to particular parts of the courtyard. This can be achieved either by planting contrasting species or using large, individual specimens.

style sources

classical lines

If garden making is an indicator of civilization, the ancient Romans were indeed a highly civilized people. Their gardens were fine pieces of garden art, from which you can adopt or adapt many ideas to create a modern courtyard setting.

The typical Roman urban garden, the *hortus*, was rectangular in shape and formal in layout. It was both an exterior living space and a garden, and was central to family life, for the Romans, like us, recognized the importance of quality leisure time. The most characteristic feature was the peristyle—a covered walkway running around all four sides of the perimeter. The peristyle roof created an area sheltered from sun and rain, while the low trellis panels between the pillars served as architectural picture frames for murals depicting natural scenes—rivers, woods, the sea, mountains, and so on—that inspired the design of the central open space. This area, also rectangular, was the garden proper, and could either be on the same level as the peristyle or sunk below it.

Paths, made from compacted earth in dry climates, sand and gravel in wetter ones, led to the main garden features and defined the planting areas. Evergreen box was grown as a low hedge to edge the

beds and were often clipped to form topiary shapes. Within the beds, seasonal flowers added variety. The species grown were those native to Italy or originating from provinces within the Roman Empire, and were therefore mainly Mediterranean and European in origin. Many plants were grown specifically to be made into the wreaths and garlands used in religious and public ceremonies, holidays, and feast days. Those most favored were roses and violets.

A common feature was the central water basin. Various designs have been uncovered, ranging from the simple to the flamboyant, but most were based on a rectangle shape and were sunk into the ground. The basin's lining varied from plain concrete to a bright blue plaster render (the color of a modern swimming pool), or even an ornate mosaic inlay. There was often a fountain set within the basin, the water emerging from a bowl, urn, or statue. When the fountain was not running, the still water reflected the sky and statuary: when the fountain was working the sound of falling water could be heard throughout the garden (Today, water pumps mean that such effects are available at the flick of a switch, whereas the Romans had to rely on gravity to power their waterworks.)

A more entertaining use of water was afforded by the water stairs, often incorporated into another popular and charming feature, the *nymphaeum aediculae*. Positioned against an outside wall, this was an ornate shrine or small temple covered with bright, geometric

mosaic patterns and shells, and dedicated to one of the deities associated with the garden. There were also decorative items made from colorful materials such as stone, marble, terracotta, bronze, and mosaic. Pieces were selected to honor the gods and goddesses associated with the garden: for example, Venus as the protectress of the *hortus* and Pan as the god of nature and the universe. *Herms*, busts of a deity on a pillar like shaft, were popular, perhaps because they would have been less expensive than a full statue.

Seats and tables for entertaining were made of carved stone or bronze and stone. A most ingenious idea was the cushion-covered, stone water couch—elegant and ornamental, yet practical. Water couches were arranged around the pool, in which the wine would be immersed to keep it cool.

A classical garden is suitable for all but the coldest regions. However, as a full peristyle would be expensive, the plan overleaf shows a covered walkway at one

The artist's impression (left) of the corner of a Roman town garden depicts a small fountain and a shady covered walkway decorated with garlands of flowers, with trellis panels between the pillars. The sunken courtyard is paved in a pattern of mosaic tiles.

An atmosphere of crumbling antiquity (opposite and below) is carefully contrived by the Roman arch set in a "collapsing" wall and the dominant tall Greek columns. The fallen petals, ivy-clad walls, lichen-covered bust, and weeds growing up through the flooring heighten this feeling, while the ornate table implies outdoor dining.

The weathered bust (below)—viewed here from a different angle—evokes a sense of aged elegance. The floor is edged with a Greek key design, which draws the eye to the mound of box, a favorite plant that was often clipped into topiary shapes.

end of the courtyard. Supported on Roman-style pillars, it not only captures the essence of the classical garden but is also attractive yet functional. A less expensive alternative would be to mount awnings on the walls. These could be extended or folded away as the weather dictated.

A perimeter stone-flagged path and trellis work panels define and separate the walkway from the sunken central garden, which is entered down a series of steps at either end of the garden. For more growing space, you could simply make a level courtyard with larger beds and a narrower path. In this design, the beds and paths are clearly defined by a low, clipped hedge of *Buxus sempervirens* (box). The planting is traditional, but there is no reason why you should restrict yourself to this selection, as many modern species would look completely at home in a classical courtyard.

With the addition of garden lighting, the classical courtyard is a place to entertain and enjoy life in true Roman style.

A modern classic (above), in which clean lines of white concrete cast into Roman-style arches and colonnade contrast with the curvaceous statue, dramatically lit. The asymmetrical layout is theatrical, and is made even more so by minimal planting,

The rectangular pool (left) dominates this tranquil courtyard. Both the pool and the lion's-head fountain impose a structure of classical formality. The strong lines are gently softened by gravel, natural rock, and mounds of clipped evergreens.

plants for a classical courtyard

1 *Lilium candidum*

2 *Arbutus unedo*

3 *Matthiola incana*

4 *Vinca minor*

5 *Crocus sativus*

6 *Prunus laurocerasus*

7 *Asplenium scolopendium*

8 *Viola odorata*

9 *Thymus vulgaris*

10 *Lilium martagon*

11 *Myrtus communis*

12 *Artemisia arborescens*

13 *Hedera helix*

14 *Narcissus poeticus*

15 *Hesperis matronalis*

16 *Viburnum tinus*

17 *Athyrium filix-femina*

18 *Erysimum cheiri*

19 *Acanthus spinosus*

20 *Rosa* 'Madame Hardy'

21 *Rosa* x *damascena*

22 *Tanacetum parthenium*

23 *Lavandula stoechas*

24 *Lychnis flos-jovis*

25 *Buxus sempervirens*

islamic influences

Enclosed behind walls and shut off from the outside world, the Islamic courtyard garden incorporates geometric design, running water, and beautiful plants, offering a calm and shady retreat from the hustle and bustle of life.

The prophet Muhammad founded Islam in the sands of what is now Saudi Arabia and, since its establishment in the 7th century AD, Muslim conquerors have spread Islam far and wide. In the Koran, the faithful are promised that "the Garden of Paradise shall be their hospitality, therein to dwell forever." To a desert-dwelling people, references to "spreading shade," "fruit and fountains and pomegranates," "running water," and "cool pavilions" would, indeed, have seemed like paradise.

This spiritual blueprint was used to make gardens on Earth, but wherever Islamic artists made gardens, they absorbed indigenous ideas. So, while gardens as far apart as those of the Moguls in India, the Umayyad Empire in Persia, and the Moors in Spain share common Islamic traits, each has an individual style. There is plenty of evidence to show how these earthly paradises looked, including such masterpieces as the Taj Mahal in Agra, India, the Generalife in Granada, Spain, and the Agdal gardens in Marrakesh, Morocco.

As well as surviving gardens and archeological remains, there are beautiful carpets from Persia depicting gardens and painted manuscripts from Mogul India that provide records of gardens of luxuriant profusion. These tend to focus on the gardens of the great, but religious connotations were as significant to the common man as to caliphs and emperors, and small, intimate, enclosed gardens were routinely made to provide cool, calm retreats. These corners of paradise are full of ideas for making a beautiful courtyard.

Regardless of size, an Islamic garden has a geometric layout with associated symmetry. On entering through an ornate gateway, the senses are welcomed by sweet-smelling bright flowers and the sound of flowing water. A fountain or, in larger gardens, a pavilion, occupies the center of the space. Radiating away from this are four walks or rills (narrow water channels), which, representing the four rivers of life, divide the garden into quadrants—hence the Old Persian name *chahar bagh*, or "four gardens." A path of marble, stone, brick, pebbles, or mosaics provides access around the garden and defines the *chahar bagh* and the flower borders that fill the space up to the courtyard walls.

The four quadrants may be treated in a number of ways. In hot climates they are often paved with stone or marble slabs, on

Emperor Babur (opposite, top) supervises the laying out of his *chahar bagh* in this illustration from a 16th-century manuscript from Mogul India. The requisite four beds are richly planted with flowers.

The fountain of life (opposite, center), set in the middle of the courtyard, is a must in an Islamic garden. This style of scallop-edged, circular basin is typical.

The bird's eye-view of this courtyard (opposite, below) demonstrates the adaptability of the Islamic style. A small water feature ensures sufficient space for a bed of lush, oasis-like planting.

which are placed seats and potted plants. Alternatively, stone might be replaced with water, and the plant beds turned into raised pools, with a fountain in the middle of each.

In the 12th-century *chahar bagh* of the Alcazar in Seville, Spain, the flowerbeds are set 4ft below path level, creating the effect of a living garden carpet. To imitate the beautiful and exotic, jewel-like effects of a living carpet in your own garden, you can sink the flowerbeds to a depth of 24in and

A pavilion of roses (above) creates a sweetly scented, shady retreat. The ornate fountain is surrounded by decorative tiling, and is approached by gravel paths rather than the traditional water rills that divide the Islamic garden into the four quarters, as described in the Koran..

fill them with low-growing bulbs and perennials, using annuals for additional touches of color during the summer. For a more verdant effect, fill each quarter with lawn, and you will then have the option of planting the grass with bulbs.

plants for an islamic courtyard

1 *Chamaerops humilis* 2 *Jasminum officinale*
3 *Rosa hemisphaerica* 4 *Platanus orientalis*
5 *Rosa moschata* 6 *Prunus cerasus* 7 *Myrtus communis* 8 *Prunus persica* 9 *Morus nigra*
10 *Cydonia oblonga* 11 *Rosa rubiginosa*
12 *Citrus limon* 13 *Citrus aurantium* 14 *Prunus avium* 15 *Prunus dulcis* 16 *Cercis siliquastrum*
17 *Punica granatum* 18 *Tamarix gallica*
19 *Juniperus communis* 'Hibernica'
20 *Anemone coronaria* 21 *Colchicum autumnale* 22 *Crocus biflorus* 23 *Crocus sativus* 24 *Hyacinthus orientalis* 25 *Inula helenium* 26 *Lilium martagon* 27 *Lilium monadelphum* 28 *Myosotis sylvatica*
29 *Narcissus poeticus* 30 *Papaver somniferum*
31 *Smyrnium olusatrum* 32 *Tulipa humilis*
33 *Tulipa linifolia* Batalini Group 'Red Gem'
34 *Tulipa turkestanica* 35 Grass

The courtyard plan shows a *chahar bagh* with a central fountain. Water is caught in a basin at the fountain's foot and flows along four rills into ornamental bowls, each of which contains a small bubbling fountain.

To increase the courtyard's usable space, the quadrants are planted as grass plats (plots), which could be studded with spring- and fall-flowering bulbs. For a more ornate garden, plant a flowering shrub or fruit bush in the center of each quarter. A simple but attractive alternative is to plant a narrow bed between path and lawn, and back it with a low box hedge.

Specimen conifers in black pots mark the four outer corners, and the paths are paved with white stone. The perimeter borders are planted with species that soften the garden's geometry and combine beauty with utility. *Jasminum officinale* cloaks the walls and its flowers perfume the air, as do the citrus blossom and the roses. Fruit trees—*Morus nigra* (mulberry), *Prunus dulcis* (almond), *Cydonia oblonga* (quince), *Prunus persica* (peach), and *Punica granatum* (pomegranate)—produce their edible bounty, while ornamental shrubs such as *Myrtus* (myrtle), *Cercis siliquastrum* (Judas tree), *Cupressus* (cypress), and *Tamarix* (tamarisk) add form, texture, and color. The two *Platanus orientalis* (Oriental plane), will be allowed to grow tall enough

The elevated pavilion, embellished with couch, drapery, and a raised water feature, evokes the exotic atmosphere of the Arabian Nights. An avenue of orange trees, flanked by twin rills, creates a setting reminiscent of the Generalife in Granada, Spain.

to shade the seat before they need to be pruned. Shade near the house is provided by an extendable awning.

Bulbs and herbaceous perennials in the garden include hyacinths and tulips in spring; lilies and poppies in summer; and crocus in the fall. In a traditional Islamic garden, many plants have an allegorical meaning. So additional introductions could include *Rosa rubinginosa* (eglantine) as a symbol for the face, an apple for the chin, and juniper for the figure of one's beloved.

medieval ideas

The medieval garden is a breath of fresh air—a safe haven within which are sweet-smelling herbs and flowers, intimate bowers, bubbling fountains, and romantic, flowery meads.

The medieval pleasure garden of the late 11th century represents the dawn of a new gardening age in northern Europe. It developed its own style, but much of the inspiration came from excursions into Moorish Spain and from the Crusades, which began in 1095. The Normans, in particular, exposed for the first time to Islamic garden art and plants, brought new ideas back with them. "Flowery meads" and a fascination with water features, for example, were Islamic in origin, while the great royal hunting parks were distant cousins of the Assyrian *pairidaeza* (the origin of the word "paradise.")

The ornamental garden or "herber" was made within the safety of castle walls, for peace was fragile. Sometimes referred to

as the *hortus conclusus*, literally an "enclosed garden," its prime use was for entertaining and repose, often becoming a setting for romantic dalliance in the privacy of a fragrant bower. Yet its design is much less sophisticated than the garden of the enemy that so influenced its features. Often square or oblong in shape, and screened from the rest of the castle by trellis, the layout lacked geometry or symmetry. Indeed, the charm and the intricacies behind the apparent simplicity of the medieval garden are its modesty, and the diversity of ways in which the distinctive features can be arranged.

Medieval courtyards often contained a flowery mead—a lawn sown with many low-growing flowers. In larger gardens, the mead included fruit trees, creating a *viridarium* or ornamental orchard. In contrast, the grass-free courtyard was given over to raised rectangular beds linked by intersecting gravel or paved paths. Made from wood or brick, raised beds are a practical solution for a confined space. They add structure and a change in level; all-round access allows ease of maintenance, and the soil is kept in the bed, and not tracked indoors.

Planting arrangements were not prescribed, and in contrast with monastic beds, where typically one species was grown in each bed, the mix of flowers, shrubby species, and herbs was simply blended to create an ornamental effect. The range of plants available in medieval times was very limited, compared to what is available today, and most plants fulfilled several roles. As well as contributing beauty, many of the plants and herbs grown had medicinal and culinary uses, or were strewn on interior floors as primitive air fresheners. Sweet-scented flowers and herbs were also made into

Wooden trellis panels (left) smothered with roses enclose a scented retreat. The simple design of this 15th-century castle garden includes a lawn and turf seats reached through a wooden gateway. The gateway leads from a vine-clad trellis tunnel lined with raised beds.

A circular seat (right) of woven willow wands in a French monastery garden is enclosed by apple trees trained against a willow trellis. Profuse planting reflects the medieval skill of arranging together plants with a medicinal or culinary use in order to create a highly ornamental display.

nosegays (small bouquets) and held to the nose when outside in order to mask the unpleasantness of everyday odors.

Grass or no grass, the medieval garden included ornamental features such as trellis work—used as panels on the walls or formed into tunnels—and fountains. And since honey was much valued as a sweetener and as an essential ingredient in the manufacture of mead, bee skeps (straw bee hives) were also extremely popular. Bowers became fashionable in the 12th century as a result of royal romantic intrigue. Made of willow withies or live sapling trees tied together and cloaked with climbers such as roses, ivy, grape vines, honeysuckle, *Clematis* species, and *Jasminum officinale*,

the bower provided a sheltered, private seating area that was perfect for "intimacy."

The medieval courtyard design combines aspects of both styles. To set the scene, the boundary is painted to look like castle walls, while near the house is the flowery mead. The mead is planted with two fruit trees as a reminder of the *viridarium*, and also boasts the ornamental fountain, which would be equally in keeping as a focal point within a garden of raised beds. Against the wall is another medieval favorite, the chamomile seat, which releases its lovely fragrance when sat on. Additional features could be perimeter flowerbeds, wall-mounted trellis panels covered with climbers, or a turf maze, in which the

pattern cut in the grass symbolizes the tortuous route through life to final salvation.

The trellis screen, smothered with fragrant roses, divides the two areas. Behind it is the *hortus conclusus*, entered through an *allée* of pleached *Carpinus betulus* (hornbeams). This is a living alternative to a pergola-tunnel made from trellis work and covered with climbing plants. Set within the gravel flooring are the traditionally planted raised beds, with the ornamental bee skep on a table. The live willow bower will give structure in the winter, and when it is in full leaf it will provide a shady, green retreat. The chamomile planted on the floor echoes the chamomile seat, and will perfume the air when it is walked on.

In this secret garden (left), contrasting shades of green act as a foil to the solidity of the water feature and the woodwork plant pyramid. The tranquillity can be enjoyed from a climber-clad willow bower.

plants for a medieval courtyard

1 *Stachys officinalis* **2** *Colchicum autumnale* **3** *Oenothera biennis* **4** *Symphytum officinale* **5** *Mentha* x *piperita* **6** *Foeniculum vulgare* **7** *Primula veris* **8** *Viola tricolor* **9** *Papaver somniferum* **10** *Santolina chamaecyparissus* **11** *Ocimum basilicum* **12** *Osmorhiza longistylis* **13** *Myrtus communis* **14** *Anethum graveolens* **15** *Rosmarinus officinale* **16** *Chamaemelum nobile* **17** *Lonicera periclymenum* **18** *Jasminum officinale* **19** *Ruta graveolens* **20** *Allium ursinum* **21** *Tanacetum cinerariifolium* **22** *Cynara cardunculus* **23** *Thymus vulgaris* **24** *Origanum majorana* **25** *Mentha spicata* **26** *Verbena officinalis* **27** *Lavandula angustifolia* **28** *Tanacetum vulgare* **29** *Allium sativum* **30** *Origanum vulgare* **31** *Angelica archangelica* **32** *Laurus nobilis* **33** *Hyssopus officinalis* **34** *Allium schoenoprasum* **35** *Rosa* x *damascena* var. *versicolor* **36** *Rosa gallica* 'Versicolor' **37** *Rosa glauca* **38** *Carpinus betulus* **39** *Malus domestica* **40** *Mespilus germanica* **41** *Agrostemma githago* **42** *Bellis perennis* **43** *Convallaria majalis* **44** *Crocus purpureus* **45** *Dactylorhiza majalis* **46** *Echium vulgare* **47** *Geranium sanguineum* **48** *Hyacinthoides non-scripta* **49** *Lamium galeobdolon* **50** *Linaria purpurea* **51** *Narcissus pseudonarcissus* **52** *Orchis mascula* **53** *Papaver rhoeas* **54** *Phlomis fruticosa* **55** *Pilosella aurantiaca* **56** *Primula vulgaris* **57** *Pulsatilla vulgaris* **58** *Silene dioica* **59** *Veronica chamaedrys* **60** *Vicia cracca* **61** *Viola odorata*

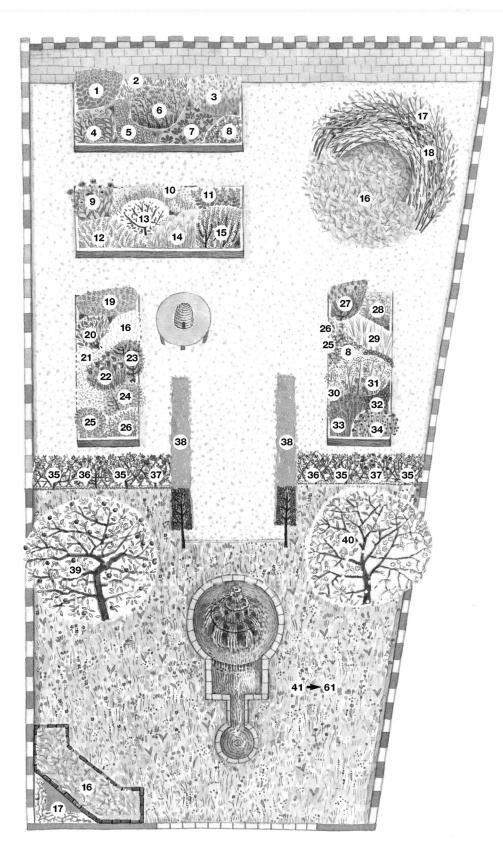

renaissance
artifice

The Italian Renaissance garden represents a high point in Western garden art, which at the time influenced garden design across the whole of Europe. As a source of inspirational ideas for the courtyard, it is as relevant today as it was innovative more than five centuries ago.

Ornate garden buildings, intricate water features, fine statuary, evergreen trees, and bright flowers filled the Italian Renaissance garden. This was an elaborate work of art, a place to impress visitors, to entertain and discuss with guests the newly rediscovered classical writings of ancient Greece and Rome. The garden was planned as an intrinsic part of the house, and the two were linked by a series of terraces and a ground plan based on symmetry. The garden's main axis ran from the doorway in the center of the house to the end of the garden; the areas to right and left of this line were essentially mirror images. Within this architectural framework grew many newly introduced plants, including *Agave* species and *Capsicum annuum* from the New World, and bulbs from Persia and the Levant, as well as species familiar to Roman gardeners.

The influence of the Renaissance garden spread across all of Europe, with each country interpreting its concepts in a slightly different way. It reached England in the mid to late 16th century where, enclosed behind the protective walls of the typical manor house, it evolved on a smaller scale than its European cousins, as a hybrid of Italian, French, and wholly English ideas. This hybrid has much to offer the modern courtyard gardener. From Italy and France came the terrace, central axis, garden buildings such as gazeboes, water features, and statues, as well as menageries, aviaries, and grottoes, plants such as *Acanthus mollis* (bear's breeches), *Lilium martagon* and *Syringa* x *persica* (lilac). From England came sundials and mounts (high mounds of earth). Surmounted by a seat or summerhouse, the mount offered a vantage point from which to look out over the garden's protective walls. New plants brought back from North America by English adventurers included *Solidago canadensis* (goldenrod), *Lobelia cardinalis*, and *Actaea rubra* (baneberry). And there were knot gardens. Although the first reference to these is found in an Italian book published in 1499, it was the English who took the idea to heart and developed it.

Knot gardens are features that work particularly well in the small space of a contemporary courtyard. They are beautiful, self-contained, provide all-year structure, and have a fascinating ancestry. Within a square bed or series of beds, the pattern of a knot is picked out using low hedges of box, *Santolina*, or *Armeria* (thrift). The gaps in between are filled with colored gravel or planted with flowers, many of which would have been familiar to the medieval gardener, and continued the principle of planting for beauty and utility. However, the Renaissance arrangement is more ornamental, with flowering perennials and annuals planted in clumps to make an informal tapestry of color and scent that changes with the seasons. Early knots had simple geometric patterns, such as a square divided into four symmetrically shaped quarters, but as time went by the patterns became more and more intricate. In a larger courtyard, the whole knot area could be enclosed by a low trellis fence, known as "railing in" the garden.

The axially-arranged plan on page 31 picks up on the idea of Italian symmetry. The stone-flagged upper terrace is a place to sit and contemplate the universe, or to entertain. The atmosphere is relaxing—there is the gentle sound of a small water feature, and the perfume of white and red roses that cloak the walls. An ornate balustrade separates the upper and lower terraces, with steps

A wisteria-smothered column (opposite) and lichen-encrusted sculpture frame the view to a balustraded terrace, evoking the timeless elegance of an Italian Renaissance garden. The style combines strong architectural features and ornaments with soft, flowering plants.

A graceful water nymph (above right) in a grotto entices you to visit her watery bower, set in a terrace wall covered with water-washed cobblestones.

Horology (right) was a Renaissance obsession, and the shape and intricate structure of the armillary sphere sundial is picked up in the planting and the overall pattern in this tiny but charming courtyard. The use of gravel to fill the knot beds helps to reduce maintenance.

plants for a renaissance courtyard

1 *Quercus ilex* **2** *Iris germanica* **3** *Daphne mezereum* **4** *Vinca minor* **5** *Convallaria majalis* **6** *Cynara cardunculus* **7** *Helleborus niger* **8** *Santolina chamaecyparissus* **9** *Lilium martagon* **10** *Artemisia abrotanum* **11** *Geranium sanguineum* **12** *Onopordum acanthium* **13** *Fragaria vesca* **14** *Narcissus pseudonarcissus* **15** *Hypericum androsaemum* **16** *Polygonatum odoratum* **17** *Ruta graveolens* **18** *Primula vulgaris* **19** *Ilex aquifolium* **20** *Lathyrus sylvestris* **21** *Arbutus unedo* **22** *Geranium sylvaticum* **23** *Lavandula stoechas* **24** *Thymus vulgaris* **25** *Allium schoenoprasum* **26** *Laurus nobilis* **27** *Pulmonaria officinalis* **28** *Rosmarinus officinalis* **29** *Paeonia lactiflora* 'White Wings' **30** *Artemisia absinthum* **31** *Galanthus nivalis* **32** *Euonymus europaeus* **33** *Dianthus caryophyllus* **34** *Iris* 'Florentina' **35** *Rosa x damascena* var. *versicolor* **36** *Ajuga reptans* **37** *Cistus salviifolius* **38** *Lilium pyrenaicum* **39** *Lavandula angustifolia* **40** *Viola odorata* **41** *Humulus lupulus* **42** *Buxus sempervirens* **43** *Chamaemelum nobile* **44** *Nymphaea* 'Marliacea Albidum' **45** *Rosa* 'Madame Hardy' **46** *Rosa gallica* var. *officinalis*

The Stoke Edith tapestry (above) includes the essential elements of the enclosed Renaissance garden of the 16th century: terracing with steps and ornate balastrading, gravel paths, topiary, statues, and fountains. Fruit trees, underplanted with lilies, are trained against the brick walls.

leading down to the lower terrace. In the center is a maze mosaic copied from a labyrinth in Chartres Cathedral, France—a reminder of the Renaissance garden's medieval ancestry. Around it is the knot garden, of an early, simple design.

The planting is traditional, but includes four taller focal plants in each square, which introduce height and structure. For a more restrained effect, fill each bed with a single species, such as *Dianthus* or *Ruta graveolens*, and for a colorful, modern display plant the beds with seasonal bedding such as *Lobelia*, *Calceolaria*, *Impatiens*, or *Salvia*.

As an alternative, you could turn a knot garden into an ornamental herb garden or, in order to keep maintenance to a minimum, fill the compartments with different colored gravels instead of with flowering plants. Gravel used in this way is particularly effective if the knot is complex.

To introduce additional eye-catching focal points, the center of each quarter could feature a popular Renaissance feature such as topiary, a statue, a fountain, an heraldic beast, a sundial, or a specimen conical conifer, for example *Juniperus communis* 'Hibernica.' Another change of level can be introduced by adding a miniature mount as a plinth for a statue, fountain, or sundial. If your courtyard is larger than the one in the plan, you could create more than one knot, rail in the knot, or add a gazebo.

japanese inspiration

The Japanese style incorporates natural elements with grace, simplicity, and beauty. Rocks, water, and plants are the essential elements that create an elegant yet virtually maintenance-free courtyard garden suitable for a range of climates.

The Western world first became excited by the beauty of eastern decorative arts, including gardens, in the 18th century. Oriental garden design broke away from the strict formality of western design that was then in vogue. This affair with the East continued throughout the 19th century, especially when beautiful new plants such as acers, azaleas, bamboos, and magnolias began to make their way to the West. By the turn of the 20th century, creating Japanese gardens had become an established fashion, which continues today as we seek the calm beauty and spiritual significance that is inherent in Oriental design.

While no one but the Japanese and Chinese can create gardens with their full religio-philosophical significance, we can look to the East for inspiration. The ancient Japanese religion of Shintoism assumes nature is on a par with humans, and is therefore respected. Following this belief, traditional gardens pay homage to and embellish the rich, beautiful landscape, and are created to form an extension of nature. The hard, rough, unmoving rocks, used in groups of three, five, and seven, or arranged together to create false mountains, harmonize with the other main element—fluid, reflective water.

The idea of opposites comes from the Chinese concept of yin and yang, the two elemental forces believed to lie behind all creation. It is an effective concept to use in designing the layout of a courtyard garden, for progression—from sun to shade, elevation to depression, wide to narrow, water to rock—provides continual change and variety within a small space.

Plants are grown for beauty and form rather than horticultural novelty. They add to the garden structure—azaleas are often clipped to look like rocks, moss provides lush ground cover, ferns rise taller, and small fruit trees, shrubs, conifers, camellias, and rhododendrons add further height, while elegant bamboos pierce the sky. Color, scent, and blossom also play an important role throughout the seasons. As spring gives way to summer, a flowering canopy of plum, peach, and cherry trees loses its petals, creating a carpet of fallen blossoms. Then fragrant *Wisteria*, *Syringa* (lilac), and *Plumeria* (frangipani) take over before the fall show of leaves and *Chrysanthemum*—the Japanese national flower.

The harmony of natural materials and plants creates the setting for manufactured ornaments. Bamboo and

The traditional oriental garden (top) takes its inspiration from nature. Trees are an essential element in the design and are carefully positioned to achieve the desired effect. They frequently have a very sculptural form, as illustrated here in this fine Japanese watercolor.

The use of natural and manufactured materials (above) creates a varied yet harmonious setting in a landscaped courtyard heavily influenced by traditional eastern ideas of gardening. The success of the design lies in the overriding note of informality while following a prescribed plan.

East meets West (right) in the otherwise unforgiving habitat of a conurbation—truly an oasis of grace amid a rather unrelenting wall of bricks. The soft, undulating carpet along the stream is the moss-like *Selaginella,* a tender plant for damp, humid conditions. Lamps have been thoughtfully placed near the steps to the tea house to illuminate the way.

heather screens are used to block views and generate a sense of mystery and surprise. Stone bridges cross pools and streams, deer scarers add sound, and stone lanterns light your way to the tea house where, just before entering and experiencing the tea ceremony, you purify yourself with water from a stone bowl. The Japanese garden style benefits from lighting that accentuates the architectural shapes of many features and plants, as well as casting entrancing shadows, especially when the wind blows.

The plan overleaf, which shows a courtyard requiring very little maintenance, incorporates eastern features arranged in an harmonious way. The crazy-paving path, with red pointing between the stones, makes a sinuous approach to the bamboo screens that divide the courtyard in two. The features are not ornate and this simplicity is in keeping with the raked gravel and water feature. The stone lantern lights the way, and you are drawn forward as the stone path disappears in the distance, generating a sense of anticipation—what is on the other side?

Turning the corner, there is the surprise of another garden. This area has a more enclosed atmosphere. A curved path of raised stepping stones—a traditional

effect—approaches the tea house, which is first glimpsed above the rock. The change from hard-edged paving to stepping stones adds variety, while continuity is retained by the use of the same rock and gravel. In a larger space, another effective way of dividing areas is to use a brick wall into which a circular moon gate is set. Equally, a large informal pool surrounded by rock, and with an unpainted, wooden, arched bridge, is a very effective feature.

The planting is uncomplicated and elegant. There are the requisite "three friends of winter": the bamboo, the pine, and the plum (in this case a cherry). Acers introduce horizontal form and striking fall foliage, while the table of bonsai set against the house wall, and an evergreen Chusan palm, *Trachycarpus fortunei*, enhance the garden's sense of stability and permanence. At night, kerosene flares impart an ethereal feel, especially the waving flames in the far garden, seen through the bamboo screen.

plants for a japanese courtyard

1 *Pinus bungeana*

2 *Acer palmatum* var. *dissectum*
   Atropurpureum Group

3 *Chimonobambusa quadrangularis*

4 *Acer palmatum* var. *dissectum*

5 *Phyllostachys nigra*

6 *Trachycarpus fortunei*

7 *Adiantum venustum*

8 *Asplenium trichomane*

9 *Osmunda regalis*

10 *Polystichum setiferum*

Dramatically-shaped rocks
(opposite, top) are surrounded by
soft moss and carefully positioned
in a bed of raked gravel, creating a
restful and uncomplicated
composition. Less can be more,
even in the smallest space.

The artless simplicity (far left)
of this gate belies its significance.
A visually arresting feature in its own
right, it also subdivides an already
small garden without blocking the
view, so that the garden retains the
unity of the overall design.

Viewed from the interior (left),
the tiny courtyard is an integral part
of the house, and demonstrates
that even the smallest space can be
transformed into a Japanese
courtyard by selecting plants and
materials on an appropriate scale.

southern
colonial spirit

Spirited pioneers who made new lives in the New World also created elegant gardens. The formal, symmetrical layouts of Southern Colonial gardens, with their emphasis on practicality, beauty, and adaptability, are perfectly suited to modern life.

Throughout the late 18th and 19th centuries, as Britain established colonies in all parts of an expanding empire, and the fledgling United States of America confirmed itself as an independent nation, intrepid settlers in the New World made gardens. The colonial garden captures the pioneer spirit, a poignant blend of reminders of home and a palpable sense of the excitement of discovery. The best known colonial courtyard gardens are in Williamsburg, Virginia, where the historic 18th-century heart of the town has been restored, and stands as a monument to the triumph of the early settlers. And the garden style that became fashionable offers today's courtyard gardener the ideal balance of usefulness and attractiveness.

In 18th-century Britain, where the landscape movement was all the rage, Capability Brown was creating vast vistas that looked more natural than nature's own. In contrast, the colonial garden was intimate and formal. Here, nature was tamed, trimmed, and kept in order. Often rectangular or square in shape, and enclosed within a hedge or a white-painted post-and-rail fence, the garden layout echoes the Anglo-Dutch style, popular in Europe in the late 1600s. A wooden veranda or porch edged with a white-painted, patterned wooden balustrade, provides a sheltered place to sit. Steps lead down to the ornamental garden, where paths of brick or gravel define geometrically-shaped and symmetrically-arranged beds, habitually edged with low hedges of *Buxus sempervirens* (box) and the dwarf variety *B. s.* 'Suffruticosa.' Beds edged with box also lined the garden perimeter, and often contained low trellis work panels supported away from the fence, against which apples were trained.

Mixed plantings of indigenous American species and European imports softened the regularity of the garden layout. In spring, the beds and borders were a riot of color as bulbs such as hyacinth, crocus, tulips, narcissus, *Anemone coronaria*, *Muscari comosum* (grape hyacinth), and *Scilla siberica* (squill) burst into flower. Summer saw a profusion of *Dianthus* (pinks), *Consolida* (larkspur), *Alcea* (hollyhock), *Digitalis* (foxglove), and roses—all introduced from England—and the American *Gaillardia*, *Coreopsis*, and *Phlox*. This informally arranged planting and the widespread use of wood, soft colored brick, and clipped evergreens introduced a rustic feel that emphasized the restricted use of ornamentation in the form of topiaried evergreens that added form and height.

Garden buildings were functional: the brick well-head, from which water was drawn for the house, was protected by a pretty wooden tiled structure, while the outside privy was housed in a small wooden shed, painted white. Clearly such practical features are superfluous in a modern colonial garden, but their form can be

adapted to modern needs. The privy can become a garden shed or an outside office, or even be replaced by a wood-frame greenhouse, while the well-head could be left as a reminder of the past, exchanged for another period feature such as a hand pump or a seat, or replaced by a modern sculpture to bring the garden up to date.

By the same token, the traditional post-and-rail fence may not provide the level of privacy that we so prize today. Another colonial style, the closepicket fence with decoratively finished slats, offers a midway alternative, but if you want complete seclusion, a 6ft white-painted, wooden closeboard fence, like that shown on the plan overleaf, will completely screen the garden from neighbors while creating a colonial atmosphere.

Lavender provides a fragrant approach (above) through the garden to the front door. The foliage and flower color contrast nicely with the herringbone brick path, a traditional flooring material also commonly laid in a header bond.

An 18th century painting (left) shows the low, white-painted picket fence and gate typical of the perimeter boundaries used to enclose Southern Colonial gardens. A veranda, from which to view the garden, was another popular feature.

Geometry and symmetry (opposite) are the key words in designing a Southern-Colonial-style courtyard. Even a small space can be given this treatment, particularly if low box hedges are filled with brightly colored flowers.

The plan shows a view of the garden from a wooden raised veranda or porch in traditional style. This could be replaced with wooden decking shaded by an awning. An appropriate addition to this area would be a twin swing seat. The paths are brick, laid in running bond, and to reduce maintenance, the edging of box along the beds has been replaced with an edging of bricks, set on end and inserted into the ground at an angle of 45 degrees, creating a saw-toothed effect. The privy has become a tool shed, while a seat, from which you can look back up the garden to the house, has replaced the well-head.

Plants are also used as features. In the central bed is a beautiful *Gymnocladus dioica* (Kentucky coffee tree), and each of the four flanking beds contains topiary cones of box. For variety, you could exchange these for artistic wooden plant supports and smother them in climbers such as *Gelsemium sempervirens* (Carolina jasmine) or *Decumaria barbara*. As tradition dictates, the planting is a mixture of species that gives year-round structure and seasonal flowerings, with the color theme in the various borders comprising whites, blues, yellows, pinks, and reds. However, it would be feasible to plant the beds using North American species only; and since the settlers also grew their own produce, a colonial courtyard could be modernized by including more fruit and adding vegetables to the beds.

An ornate gateway (right) doubles as a climber-clad wooden arch. Adapting one feature to fulfill two or more roles is an ingenious way of maximizing interest.

The shady veranda (below right) is a peaceful and sheltered area in which to sit and entertain friends.

The central water feature (below), the division of the planting area into four beds, and the tiled floor are reminiscent of the Islamic garden, an example of how similar ideas appear in different historical guises.

plants for a colonial courtyard

1 *Malus domestica*

2 *Achillea millefolium*

3 *Kalmia latifolia*

4 *Asarum canadense*

5 *Dianthus caryophyllus*

6 *Campsis radicans*

7 *Rosa virginiana* **8** *Hydrangea anomala ssp. petiolaris*

9 *Artemisia absinthium*

10 *Wisteria frutescens*

11 *Ilex verticillata* **12** *Paeonia lactiflora* 'White Wings'

13 *Chaenomeles speciosa*

14 *Hamamelis virginiana*

15 *Halimium* 'Susan'

16 *Lychnis chalcedonica*

17 *Dictamnus albus* (pink)

18 *Buxus sempervirens*

19 *Lupinus perennis*

20 *Aquilegia canadensis*

21 *Ajuga reptans* **22** *Iris pallida*

23 *Tradescantia virginiana*

24 *Nepeta nervosa*

25 *Dictamnus albus* (white)

26 *Veronica spicata*

27 Phlox *divaricata*

28 *Monarda* 'Croftway Pink'

29 *Stokesia laevis* (white)

30 *Thermopsis villosa*

31 *Iris pseudacorus*

32 *Gymnocladus dioica*

33 *Narcissus poeticus*

34 *Anemone coronaria*

35 *Crocus vernus*

36 *Fritillaria imperialis*

arts and crafts idyll

The early years of the 20th century saw the birth of elegant and idyllic gardens. These were profusely planted and full of interesting features that melded to form a period piece with many themes. Yet they are still perfectly suited to courtyard gardens in the early 21st century.

The gardens created by Gertrude Jekyll and Sir Edwin Lutyens heralded a new style of gardening, in which structure and planting were in perfect harmony, and construction was always based on principles of skilled craftsmanship and the use of local materials in local ways. The ethos of the Arts and Crafts garden spread far and wide, and was championed in America by Beatrix Ferrand—famous for Dumbarton Oaks—and in Australia by Edna Walling.

Such gardens were the epitome of relaxed elegance, which was achieved by the ingenious use of geometric asymmetry. Arches, brick paths, rills, and lawns, steps and pergolas, effortlessly linked a series of garden rooms enclosed by tall hedges or walls. Each garden room had its own character, based around interesting features such as terraces and changes in level, lily ponds, rose gardens, dry-stone walls, summerhouses, seats, and croquet and tennis lawns. This infrastructure, designed to maintain each feature's character while creating a unified whole, gave the Arts and Crafts courtyard its identity.

Miss Jekyll invented the idea of painting with plants—designing beds and borders for an overall color effect within which the plants would display their individual beauty. And unlike their Victorian gardening predecessors, who had a passion for bedding plants, the Arts and Crafts gardeners crammed the garden full of frost-hardy plants (although tender plants were. admissible as seasonal highlights). However, these hardy species did not have to be native. Indeed, Miss Jekyll and her followers were enthusiastic users of plants brought back from the four corners of the globe by those extraordinary adventurer-botanists, the plant hunters. In the early 1900s, western China was yielding up its treasures to men such as George Forrest, Ernest Wilson (later keeper of Harvard's Arnold Arboretum), and Frank Kingdon-Ward. Wonderful new bulbs, such

A riot of color (above), created by the massed planting of herbaceous perennials, softens the strong architectural form of the hard landscaping, while the stone archway frames the garden beyond.

The wrought iron gate (opposite, far left) provides a focal structural element. The close planting demonstrates the stunning effects that can be created by the careful arrangement of form, color and texture.

The painting of Gertrude Jekyll's garden (opposite, left), Munstead Wood, near Godalming, England, illustrates her use of plants to "paint" garden pictures. Miss Jekyll paid great attention to detail, particularly to the way in which foliage and flower colors were arranged in bed and border.

as *Lilium regale*, shrubs and trees such as *Viburnum*, *Camellia*, *Davidia involucrata* and *Rhododendron*, perennials such as *Primula burmanica*, and climbers such as *Clematis armandii* and, of course, *Parthenocissus tricuspidata* (Boston ivy), brightened the Arts and Crafts garden and added a touch of the exotic. So, whether herbaceous borders, rockeries, shrubberies, or annual displays, the beds and borders were planted with a profuse and diverse flowering display, their apparent artlessness belying the highly organized and carefully orchestrated planning.

Artistic planting, a variety of features and the various ways they can be arranged together make the Arts and Crafts garden an ideal inspiration for a courtyard. However, associated as they were with large country houses, for the courtyard gardener there is a golden rule – avoid the temptation to cram a quart into a pint container. Temper exuberance by making a wish list of features and then exercise self-control as you match garden space with desired effect. With a bit of imagination, you will be surprised at what you can fit into a small space while retaining the ambience of the golden afternoons enjoyed by previous generations. Remember, also, that certain features can be shrunk more easily than others. For example, a couple of square yards of well designed and

Plants tumbling onto a curved path (above) create a very gentle, country cottage look. This reverence for local materials, using the traditional skills of the craftsman and old-fashioned plants, were core values of the Arts and Crafts movement.

Charming, small garden buildings (below) were popular structural additions to the Arts and Crafts garden. So, too, were. pergolas, sunken lily ponds, rockeries, and stone paths.

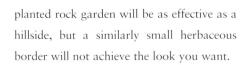

planted rock garden will be as effective as a hillside, but a similarly small herbaceous border will not achieve the look you want.

The plan shows a central sunken garden with lily pond and fountain, flanked by drystone walls and separated from the borders by tall yew hedges. As well as providing access to the pool, a network of paths links all areas of the garden, including the pergola and summerhouse.

With the main features arranged, the next issue is the planting. In the spirit of the Arts and Crafts garden, the borders have distinct seasonal displays —a spring border, a summer herbaceous border, and a fall shrub border. Your aim in arranging the plants should be to emulate Miss Jekyll and paint a picture with plants using organized color coordination. Admittedly, it is much harder to do than it seems, because you need to consider not just flower color, but flowering time, plant height, foliage color, and shape, as well as the way in which these attributes will fit with neighboring plants and contribute to the overall picture.

Practice is the only way to perfect the art, but it helps to know that Miss Jekyll always planted in informal, bold, sweeping groups or swathes, and in small garden compartments she regularly planted the beds using only one or two colors. However, in long herbaceous borders, Miss Jekyll often began the color theme with cool colors (blues, mauves, and whites), then built to a crescendo of hot colors (reds, oranges, and yellows) in the middle before cooling down again at the far end.

plants for an arts and crafts courtyard

1 *Parthenocissus tricuspidata*

2 *Rosa* 'Gloire de Dijon'

3 *Clematis* 'Nellie Moser'

4 *Vitis coignetiae*

5 *Wisteris sinensis* 'Alba'

6 *Jasminum officinale*

7 *Clematis montana* 'Elizabeth'

8 *Helleborus niger*

9 *Primula vulgaris*

10 *Narcissus* 'Tête-à-Tête'

11 *Erythronium americanum*

12 *Crocus tommasinianus*

13 *Narcissus* 'Cheerfulness'

14 *Chinodoxa forbesii* 'Pink Giant'

15 *Erythronium dens-canis*

16 *Bulbocodium vernum*

17 *Tulipa saxatilis*

18 *Erythronium californicum*

19 *Fritillaria pallidiflora*

20 *Lilium candidum*

21 *Fritillaria meleagris*

22 *Taxus baccata*

23 *Dianthus* 'Musgrave's Pink'

24 *Lewisia rediviva*

25 *Helianthemum appeninum*

26 *Saxifraga cuneifolia*

27 *Convolvulus sabatius*

28 *Dianthus gratianopolitanus*

29 *Saxifraga sempervivum*

30 *Erysimum cheiri*

31 *Aubrieta* 'Purple Cascade'

32 *Nymphaea* 'American Star'

33 *Nymphaea* 'Marliacea Albida'

34 *Allium cristophii*

35 *Campanula latiloba*

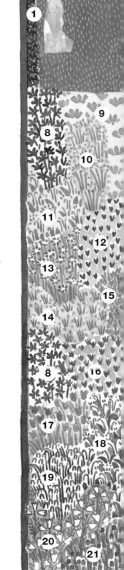

36 *Eryngium bourgatii*

37 *Nepeta nervosa*

38 *Gypsophilla paniculata* 'Bristol Fairy'

39 *Crocosmia x crocosmiiflora* 'George Davison'

40 *Kniphofia erecta* **41** *Lilium pumilum*

42 *Hemerocallis lilioasphodelus*

43 *Delphinium* 'Butterball'

44 *Lilium* 'Connecticut King'

45 *Geranium sanguineum*

46 *Osteospermum* 'Whirligig' **47** *Yucca gloriosa*

48 *Colchicum* 'Waterlily' **49** *Fothergilla major*

50 *Viburnum x bodnantense* 'Dawn'

51 *Rhododendron yakushimanum* 'Bambi'

52 *Nerine bowdenii* var. *wellsii*

53 *Mahonia japonica*

54 *Cyclamen hederifolium*

55 *Cotinus coggygria* 'Notcutt's Variety'

56 *Prunus subhirtella* 'Autumnalis'

latin patio

The Spanish word patio means "courtyard," and the hallmarks of the Latin courtyard are bold, simple design, extravagant use of bright colors, and striking plants, all of which blend together to generate excitement.

Like seeds, garden-making ideas blow across the world and, arriving at a patch of fertile soil, they germinate and grow. But just as plants grown from seed have their own distinctive character, so new garden styles develop in new countries. The Latin courtyard is a case in point. Mexico became a Spanish colony following the defeat of the Aztecs in 1521 so, not surprisingly, the Mexican garden has a strong Spanish flavor. The story does not end there, for Spanish gardens owe much to the Islamic gardens of the North African Moors who conquered Spain in the 7th century; these gardens in turn were direct descendants of those created in Persia. Therefore, the Latin courtyard can trace its origins back some 1,300 years and across two continents.

The layout of the Latin courtyard retains traces of its ancient ancestry; many are surrounded on all sides by living areas, and a water feature is ubiquitous. However, the Latin courtyard has its own distinctive character, one dominated by a fiesta lifestyle with much of the open space dedicated to outdoor living and eating.

Bold simplicity is the key to creating a successful Latin courtyard. The structure is relatively straightforward, but the way in which it is decorated challenges everyone to have fun. There is scope to mix and match materials and floors. Walls can be constructed from terracotta or ceramic tiles, painted adobe or concrete, patterned brick, mosaics, or stone. But whatever is used, it must have a strong, bright color. Apart from the walls and floor, the most dominant feature of a Latin courtyard is the raised water basin and fountain. Often positioned in the center of the courtyard, it has a rim that is wide enough to sit on or place potted plants on. It may be plain and simply painted, or decorated with mosaics or tiles, or inlaid with shells. Other appropriate ornaments and decorative features to be positioned throughout the garden as eye-catchers are artworks of

The bright house wall (left) delineates the internal shape of the courtyard space, created by changes in level and the use of horizontal and vertical lines.

Bold planting (right) is a feature of the Latin approach to design, as illustrated in *The Patio* (1988) by the artist Fernando Botero.

Raised beds (right, center) are a typical feature of a Latin courtyard, as are terracotta tiles.

The visual impact (right, below) of the sunken courtyard is stunning. The use of straight lines is emphasized by the careful placement of objects with curved surfaces—a simple ball and pot.

pre-Spanish South American cultures in different forms: wall paintings, sculptures, carvings, mosaics.

The beds and borders are geometric in shape—ovals, circles, rectangles, and squares—and large enough to contain a bold display of plants. They are arranged in the center and around the edges of the courtyard, in no prescribed style, but once again simple is best. Ground-level beds may be unadorned or edged with white-painted rocks or colored tiles, or enclosed within low, clipped hedges of box. Raised beds, made from stone or brick, provide a change in level as well as a place on which to sit or to group pots. The beds should be full of species with strong foliage and brightly colored flowers, but do not be tempted to overdo it. Use species that will be admired in their own right, and remember that the sight of bare soil is not a crime. Don't forget to plant evergreen trees such as *Ficus benghalensis* and *Magnolia grandiflora* for shade. To add another splash of color, paint their trunks to match the floor or walls. You could also brighten stone walls by planting bougainvillea, available in many colors, from red through pink to orange and white.

plants for a latin courtyard

1 *Vanda dearei* **2** *Lavandula angustifolia* **3** *Thymus vulgaris*

4 *Allium schoenoprasum* **5** *Ocimum basilicum* **6** *Anethum graveolens*

7 *Nerium oleander* 'Hawaii'

8 *Citrus limon* **9** *Magnolia grandiflora*

10 *Ensete ventricosum* **11** *Mangifera indica* **12** *Plumeria obtusa*

13 *Dracaena marginata*

14 *Livistona chinensis*

15 *Hibiscus schizopetalus* (red)

16 *Codiaeum variegatum* var. *pictum* (red) **17** *Bracteantha bracteatum*

18 *Agave americana* 'Variegata'

19 *Erythrina crista-galli*

20 *Canna indica* (red)

21 *Anthurium andraeanum* (red)

22 *Telopea speciosissima*

23 *Tropaeolum majus* (mixed colors)

24 *Ficus benghalensis*

25 *Agapanthus* 'Headbourne Hybrid'

26 *Heliotropium arborescens*

27 *Plumbago indica*

28 *Bougainvillea* 'Barbara Karst'

29 *Pseudowintera axillaris*

30 *Pachycereus marginatus*

31 *Codiaeum variegatum* var. *pictum* (yellow) **32** *Hibiscus schizopetalus* (yellow) **33** *Hemerocallis lilio-asphodelus* **34** *Sansevieria trifasciata*

35 *Fargesia nitida* **36** *Yucca gloriosa*

37 *Allamandra* 'Golden Sprite'

38 *Strelitzia reginae*

39 Pots of various cuttings taken from the plants in the main beds

The plan takes advantage of the Latin courtyard's vivacity and traditional design, but adds a dash of the modern. The colors are primary yellows, reds, and blues (and, of course, green for the plants). The floor is concrete, which is painted a bright terracotta red, as are the door frames and stucco walls, which are painted a matching color to a height of 18in. Above this, they are painted a bright indigo blue. To maintain an uncluttered feel and a peaceful atmosphere, and as a contrast to the dark, waxy green leaves of the trees and the bright flowers, the side walls are bare, except for lighting fixtures and ironwork pot holders.

Near the house, the table and chairs are shaded by four trees. There is a mosaic of the Nazca lines spider to mark the transition into the ornamental. Other ornaments include statuary and orchids planted in a tree stump. The raised beds provide seating and are planted with reds, yellows, and oranges to contrast with the floor and walls. The shape of the beds encloses the free-standing water feature, which is lined with blue and white tiles. A purple bougainvillea has been trained against the far wall to provide a backdrop to the fountain and to signal a boundary of the garden.

The informal arrangement (above) of plants used by the Mexican artist Frida Kahlo is dominated by architectural species, and includes maize. Her garden also contains many pieces of ethnic sculpture, which provide a reminder of Mexico's pre-Conquistador history.

The rich, red wall (right, top) is the perfect backdrop for the solitary black horse – an organic, albeit temporary, sculpture.

In Frida Kahlo's garden (right) the primary color blue provides a bold setting for a range of exotic flowers, such as the deservedly popular bougainvillea.

modernist
trends

The Modernist courtyard is about self-expression. As such, it is a liberating garden style that offers the freedom to experiment. At the same time, heed should be paid to the Modernist dictum "form follows function"; that is, the courtyard should marry its roles as both an outdoor room and a place to cultivate.

A classic example of Modernist principles (above)**:** A single tree provides an architectural focus as well as casting shade; the pergola leads from one area to another; the water feature is a swimming pool; and the vivid green grass provides a contrast in color and texture to the bright red tile flooring.

This Modernist prototype (right) was created at Hyères, in France, by Gabriel Guurekian in the 1920s. The beds are pieces of sculpture in their own right. When filled with seasonal bedding plants, they add interest and variety.

Minimalism (opposite right) can be brought into a courtyard space to create a very tranquil space. The use of stone and gravel has an almost Zen-like quality, while the Islamic influenced fountain fulfills its functions of introducing a calming sound, while giving height and focus to the composition.

Modernism is the radical style of artistic expression that revolutionized every art form in the early part of the 20th century and set out to provoke a response. Paintings by Picasso, novels by Kafka, sculptures by Moore, and buildings created by Le Corbusier—all challenged the established tenets of taste and heralded a profound break with the past. The Modernist garden style took a little longer to reach maturity, coming into its own in the brave new world after 1945.

Applying the Modernist principle that the form or shape of a product should be dictated by its function or use, the inspirational designers—Thomas Church and James Rose in North America, Roberto Burle-Marx in Brazil, Sir Geoffrey Jellicoe and, more recently, John Brookes in Britain —transformed the garden. No longer a passive place in which plants grew and were to be admired, it became a dynamic living space, a room outside that people used for entertaining, sunbathing, swimming, and drying the laundry. The Modernist courtyard also became a laboratory for experimenting with ways to use new materials such as ferroconcrete, concrete paving slabs, steel, and glass. In the growing areas, plants with strong form—hostas, alliums, cordyline and phormiums—became an intrinsic part of the garden's architectural structure.

In creating the Modernist courtyard you should take full advantage of new materials and use unusual shapes, forms, and colors in exciting, innovative ways.

plants for a modernist courtyard

1 *Acer palmatum* var. *dissectum*

2 *Lavandula stoechas*

3 *Corylus avellana* 'Contorta'

4 *Pleioblastus variegatus*

5 *Camellia sasanqua*

6 *Carex elata* 'Aurea'

7 *Pinus mugo*

8 *Helictotrichon sempervirens*

9 *Ophiopogon planiscapus* 'Nigrescens'

10 *Festuca glauca*

11 *Hakonechloa macra* 'Aureola'

A purity of form (opposite, above) is created by the garden infrastructure, which uses a combination of traditional and new materials. This calm, interesting space is enlivened by the planting, which makes good use of architectural plants—a form of sculpture in their own right.

John Brookes' design (opposite, right) for a garden near London, England, was created when he was going through his linear phase, and was partly inspired by a Mondrian painting. Elements of the painting became the grass, water, paving, and beds.

You can cast concrete into any shape, use thick glass and steel to make raised flowerbeds or walls, and line water displays with mirrors. The opportunities are endless. And when planting a modern courtyard, choose plants with bold shapes or foliage and/or color, and use them as pieces of living architecture or sculpture, either as individual specimens or in mass plantings.

The plan shows a very bold modern courtyard constructed from three interlinking zones: the bed zone near the house; the water zone, which divides the garden; and the relaxation zone, deliberately situated in the far corner to compel visitors to experience the whole garden before reaching it. Each zone is constructed from dyed concrete, the three bright, vivid colors contrasting strongly. This is a versatile material that comes in a wide range of colors, and because it is dyed, it does not fade in the same way that paint does.

The layout is asymmetric and uses sudden changes of level to create bold visual effects. From the door, a sloping path descends through the bed zone with its triangular flowerbeds. To the left, they step up in three tiers, creating a pyramid effect, and on the right the reverse is true: They step down into a sunken area. As you walk down the slope the beds seem to get taller or deeper, and vice versa. The planting is for effect rather than variety, and each tier is dedicated to an individual species of ornamental grass, which will provide year-round form, color and texture. In keeping with the design of the three-tier beds, with its echoes of a winner's rostrum, the color theme is "medals"—bronze, silver, and gold.

The water zone, a feature in its own right, divides the garden. Water normally flows in one direction, but here it cascades in at both ends and disappears into the sump under the stepping stone, giving it the appearance of being in the center of a vortex. Near the house, the water also flows down a chute, a modern interpretation of a Mogul Indian feature, the *chagar*. The chute's surface is raised in the pattern of fish scales to create a series of niches over which the water tumbles in a lively way.

The shape of the relaxation zone is defined by seven circular raised beds of differing heights, and is sheltered by a plain white awning supported by stainless steel poles. The planting is simple, bold, and architectural—alternate containers are planted with tall specimen plants and mass plantings of lower-growing species to provide both screening and viewing gaps into and out of the area.

Throughout the garden lighting is used extensively. It is set into the walls to illuminate the path, in the walls of the canal to give that lovely liquid effect, and casts light upward onto the canopy and plants in the relaxation zone to draw you to it. Gas torches introduce dancing flames and shadows at night.

into the **future**

The future is exciting, and all about individual choice. Drawing inspiration from the past and present, the future garden should look forward and express your hopes and expectations.

At the beginning of the 21st century, the garden maker is in a privileged position. Never before has the media—books, magazines, television, radio, Internet, and so on—offered so much inspiration. At the same time, as the story of gardens is told, so a wealth of all-but-forgotten ideas is rediscovered and made relevant once more. This quest for knowledge liberates the mind and instills the power to reject all-embracing fashions. With it comes a new design dictum—gardens are for individuals.

To take full advantage of this diversity of opportunity, however, you must also embrace technological advances and fill your future courtyard with new materials and special effects. For example, you could incorporate a large flat-screen television into a wall and show videos to generate a particular mood. Sculptures made from materials that change color according to the temperature, or systems that send forth fire or fog, are as unusual as they are dramatic. Crushed colored glass makes a novel and colorful flooring or ground cover, while computers can be used to coordinate lights and fountain activity to create a constantly moving display.

Individuality can also be expressed through the use of garden features that have a hidden meaning. Planting arrangements, sculptures, and ornaments, such as messages carved in stone, can represent milestones in your life or indicate your views on topics as diverse as conservation, politics, or your love for a particular place or garden. Yet for all its symbolism and technology, the future courtyard must pay homage to the greatest source of inspiration of them all—nature. Indigenous plant arrangements and color schemes bring nature's inherent beauty into our everyday lives, and act as a reminder of our duty to the future: care of the environment as a whole.

Using unusual materials (above) in unusual ways is one way of creating a futuristic garden. The curved wall with its irregular pattern of holes, the large spheres, and the trunks of the palm trees all differ from the commonplace, and are made all the more eye-catching by the use of bold, contrasting colors.

Artful lighting (left) has been employed as a specific structural element in this courtyard. Putting the design principle of repetition into practice, the designer has used the lights with the containers of topiaried box to create a formal structure.

Familiar materials (opposite) used in unusual ways is another method of creating a garden full of surprises. The *fleur de lys* and shells are reminiscent of the Rococo style, but here their use is very futuristic.

The plan shows my future courtyard garden, a place I want to be. It draws me out of the house and meets my needs. A tranquil haven in which I can relax, it can be transformed into a lively space where I can eat and entertain friends. And while garden design is my profession, I do not have as much time as I would like to garden, so the layout is relatively uncomplicated and the planting low maintenance, yet there are a number of special effects and materials that introduce surprise and a sense of the unusual.

The "paved" area for sitting and entertaining is covered with thick, slightly spongy rubber matting in terracotta, ocher, and gray. To help create the garden structure and unify the layout, the same material (which is pleasant to walk on and safe for children) provides access around the garden but, for variety and to define the beds, it is edged with brick pavoirs. The raised water feature, made from glass bricks, filled with fist-sized lumps of dark blue glass and lit from below, and the large boulders provide a spot for sitting and enjoying a glass of wine. The boulders also retain the raised bed. Access is along a special feature: The specimen plants and rocks are set within a ground cover of colored glass marbles.

The garden's hidden theme is the four elements—air, water, fire, and earth. The water feature is complemented by mist produced by a mist machine, which is controlled by a timer in the house and periodically envelops unwary guests in billowing clouds of white fog. The nozzles are situated by the house door, at the

"No rules apply" (bottom left) is the one true rule of futuristic design. This garden combines classical texts etched into glass panels, which double as see-through screens, with a cast concrete infrastructure and a carefully conceived planting scheme.

The future (below) of courtyard gardens could see the complete removal of the barrier between house and garden, whereby the two are a unified whole, the courtyard becoming an interior room, but without a ceiling.

edge of the largest bed and behind the water feature. To balance the water there is fire. Fire is visually most effective from twilight, when the night air comes alive with spires of flame that encircle the outer rocks and light a path to the water feature.

The earth is home to my passion—unusual, semi-tender plants with exotic foliage; the beds are filled with a display that is elegant but unfussy. The raised bed consists of ericaceous soil for acid-loving plants, which look spectacular from the house. Architectural plants in the other beds provide focus and year-round structure, set off by herbaceous planting that also introduces seasonal variety. However, several of the species used, such as *Lapageria rosea* (Chilean bell flower) and *Hedychium gardnerianum* (Kahili ginger), are too tender to survive cold winters outside. They are planted in pots that are plunged into the beds after the last frost, and are lifted in the fall to be overwintered in the octagonal greenhouse. To complete the garden there is a hidden garden shed, in which to store the garden furniture, along with barbecue and garden tools.

plants for a futuristic courtyard

1 *Musa basjoo* **2** *Clematis armandii*

3 *Chamaerops humilis*

4 *Cardiocrinum giganteum*

5 *Dicksonia antarctica*

6 *Blechnum chilense*

7 *Adiantum pedatum*

8 *Dacrydium cupressinum*

9 *Myosotidium hortensia*

10 *Epimedium* x *versicolor*

11 *Polygonatum* x *hybridum* **12** *Isoplexis canariensis* **13** *Gunnera tinctoria*

14 *Lapageria rosea* **15** *Hosta sieboldiana*

16 *Hedychium gardnerianum*

17 *Trachelospermum jasminoides* **18** *Primula florindae* **19** *Daphne* x *burkwoodii* 'Astrid'

20 *Acer palmatum* var. *dissectum*

21 *Cordyline australis* 'Torbay Dazzler'

22 *Trillium grandiflorum* **23** *Rhododendron yakushimanum* **24** *Hosta crispula*

25 *Rhododendron* 'Elizabeth' **26** *Meconopsis betonicifolia* **27** *Camellia* x *williamsii* 'Donation'

28 *Crinodendron hookerianum*

29 *Bergenia ciliata* **30** *Echium wildpretii*

31 *Grevillea rosmarinifolia* **32** *Hosta sieboldii*

designing by theme

xeriscape

Low rainfall often produces beautiful natural landscapes, in which most of the drought-tolerant, indigenous plants are extraordinary in shape and form, and can be used to stunning effect in a courtyard. Arid gardens also have another great advantage—low rainfall means fewer weeds.

An arid area is anywhere with an especially low rainfall. The problems of gardening in such areas led to the development of xeriscape, an ecological approach to dry gardening. The aim here is to use water in a sensible way, to use plants that survive naturally in these conditions, and to make use of soil mulches such as stone to retain moisture.

The Xeriscape Movement began in Denver, Colorado, in 1981. Denver receives only 14in of rain a year, and the average low in January of 18°F compares with an average high of 88°F in July. It is therefore possible to create a xeriscape courtyard in temperature zones ranging from alpine to desert. Yet wherever you make an arid courtyard, it will give maximum interest with minimal input; it will also be low maintenance as, irrespective of climate, in dry areas the weed problems associated with wetter areas simply do not exist.

Arid areas tend to have dramatic natural scenery, striking plants, and low planting densities. When designing an arid courtyard, draw your inspiration from nature, aiming for simplicity bordering on the minimalist, as an overcomplicated arid scene will lose its intrinsic beauty. The garden structure—seating areas, walls, network of paths, changes of level, and steps—are best constructed from natural materials such as stone, or manufactured products that blend sympathetically with the natural materials. In hot, arid regions, adobe (sun-dried brick) is widely used. Covered with a clay render, it is perfect for constructing perimeter walls and raised beds, retaining walls, and even garden buildings. Terracotta tiles work in all types of climate, while rendered concrete can be cast into seats or used to line pools

or water courses. Used to cover concrete blocks, it is an ideal substitute for adobe.

Color can be employed to great effect on walls and other structures. White is popular in hot climates, but can be glaring in bright sunlight. Natural tones that match indigenous ones—ocher, cinnamon, lemon, and saffron—always look good, particularly in evening light. But if you want to be unconventional, you could use colors that clash or use bold, almost lurid colors.

Xeriscape planting should be deliberately simple but effective. Beds and borders are best covered with some form of hard material, such as crushed lava, shale, stone chips, gravel, shingle, or sand, with each architectural plant given space to deliver maximum visual impact, a point emphasized by the repeated use of a single species. Many structural plants also have very colorful and/or sweetly scented blooms that create a changing scene. Plant selection should be inspired by the local flora, but do feel at libery to make use of some of the more exotic species as well.

The plan overleaf shows a courtyard for a climate with a minimum temperature of 50°F. Throughout the xeriscape, the use of varied materials helps to define the different areas, at the same time introducing a variety of texture and color. Adjacent to the house is a terracotta-tiled patio, a transitional space between the house and the garden proper. This is a place to entertain (hence the beehive oven, a fantastic alternative to the barbecue) to enjoy the cool of the evening and to unwind. The atmosphere is made all the

Plants with bizarre forms (above) are planted sufficiently far apart to ensure that they all provide maximum impact. The raised bed introduces a change in level, and its hard, concrete geometry forges a contrast with the natural plant shapes.

Texture and contrast (opposite) are essential ingredients in the xeriscape courtyard. Here the smooth horizontal lines of the wall emphasize the regularity of the vertical, ribbed cactus and the dome of airy grass. The importance of taking sun and shade into consideration during the design process is also aptly demonstrated here.

The soft, earthy tints (left) of the house and wall are a foil for a planting display dominated by greens and blue-greens. The plants are carefully positioned to take full advantage of the slope, while their colors are emphasized by the honey hues of the boulders.

Arid meets Modernist (below) in this xeriscape courtyard. The textured concrete wall and gravel-covered bed make a minimalist setting for the three plant species. It is the lack of complication that makes such displays so effective.

create a dramatic display at night, the rocks could be spotlit, individual plants lit from below, and angled lights used to cast dramatic shadows against the walls.

The shale is a canvas on which the architectural plants are displayed. Selection is for form and color, and the species come from as far afield as South Africa and Europe. Increased seasonal variety is provided by *Dorotheanus bellidiformis* (Livingstone daisy). The plants will need dead-heading occasionally, and the pool level maintained. This minimal amount of work aside, the xeriscape courtyard gives more time for relaxing and entertaining.

more conducive to relaxation by the sound of trickling water, which also brings movement and adds a sense of the oasis to the garden. Its fluidity contrasts with the spiky shapes of the rocks and plants, but since water is a precious commodity in such a habitat, flowing water is avoided in order to minimize evaporation.

A black cinder path leads from the patio around the garden, past a seat at the far end, which looks back toward the house. Below the path a "scree" bed covered with shale (thin, palm-sized lumps of flat rock similar to slate, but reddish-gray in color) falls away toward the central, informally shaped pool, which is also lined with shale. In the center, there is a large rock, similar to those used on the raised bed. A hole drilled through the rock allows it to be used as a gentle fountain.

Retained by an adobe wall and sloping up to the adobe perimeter walls, all painted white, the shale-covered raised bed contains four large rocks. These natural sculptures are the garden's only ornament, but ethnic art would be appropriate. To

plants for a xeriscape courtyard

1 *Fremontedendron califonicum*

2 *Agave parviflora*

3 *Agapanthus* 'Albatross'

4 *Agapanthus* 'Headbourne Hybrids'

5 *Kniphofia caulescens*

6 *Bougainvillea spectabilis*

7 *Aloe vera*

8 *Romneya coulteri*

9 *Selenicereus grandiflorus*

10 *Origanum dictamnus*

11 *Ocimum basilicum*

12 *Thymus vulgaris*

13 *Pereskia aculeata*

14 *Dorotheanthus bellidiformis*

15 *Campsis radicans*

16 *Echinops spachiana*

17 *Agave americana* 'Variegata'

10 *Echium wildpretii*

19 *Opuntia robusta*

20 *Phormium* 'Sundowner'

21 *Protea cynaroides*

22 *Agave utahensis*

23 *Amaryllis belladonna*

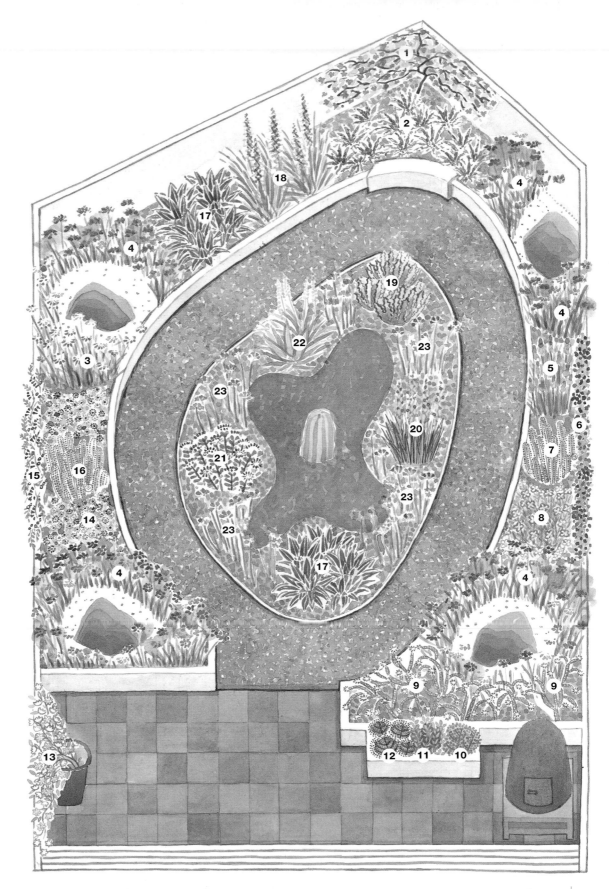

mediterranean living

The Mediterranean courtyard garden is as much about climate as it is about people and lifestyle. From a region renowned for good living comes a style that is central to family life, which has elegance born of simplicity.

The Mediterranean region has witnessed the birth of many great civilizations, and records of courtyard gardens go back millennia—even the Greek poet Homer mentions them in his epic, *The Odyssey*. However, the Mediterranean courtyard is not restricted to a geographical region. Rather it is essentially an architectural style that is appropriate to a way of living. It can be created wherever the climate consists of hot, dry summers and mild, wet winters, with the lowest temperatures rarely dropping below the freezing point. This includes parts of central and southern California, South Africa's western Cape Province, some of the coast of Chile, and parts of southern, western, and eastern Australia.

The Mediterranean courtyard is about people, and as such it has many roles to fulfill. It is a place of comfort; a quiet haven in which to begin the day; a shady retreat where you can enjoy a siesta; and a setting where family and friends gather to eat in the cool of the evening. It is also a place of practicalities—somewhere to prepare food, grow herbs for the kitchen, and provide a safe area for children to play. Above all, it is a place of beauty, its charm enhanced by an uncomplicated layout.

Typically, the walls are rendered stonework painted white, although bare stone or a mural of a Mediterranean scene are appropriate alternatives. The bright white walls often contrast with

Shades of blue (below) capture the essence of the Mediterranean style. The furniture and shelter have a rustic charm, while the elegant terracotta jar introduces a sense of civilizations long since past.

An epic scene (right) depicted in tiles not only reminds one of past glories but also introduces a decorative element to the courtyard. The gnarled vine provides a shady retreat at midday from the Mediterranean sun.

plants for a mediterranean courtyard

1 *Lavandula angustifolia* 'Alba'

2 *Lavandula stoechas* **3** *Prunus dulcis*

4 *Vitis vinifera* **5** *Olea europaea*

6 *Pelargonium* 'Voodoo'

7 *Citrus limon* **8** *Ocimum basilicum*

9 *Mentha* x *piperita* **10** *Thymus vulgaris*

11 *Origanum vulgare* ssp. *hirtum*

12 *Bougainvillea glabra* 'Singapore Beauty'

13 *Ipomoea tricolor* 'Heavenly Blue'

blue painted steps and door frames, while the floor is usually constructed of stone paving, although terracotta tiles or painted concrete are sometimes used. Features are few, and most combine a practical with an ornamental role. Near the house, a space is set with a table and chairs, while another ubiquitous feature, the shady pergola covered with plants or roofed with bamboo, may be positioned further away for privacy. A water feature is a recent but valuable addition to the traditional Mediterranean courtyard, as it introduces movement and sound; however, the design of the water feature must be simple in order to maintain the overall effect.

The planting follows this pattern of elegant and practical simplicity. Shade-giving and fruiting specimens such as *Olea europaea* (olive), *Prunus armeniaca* (apricot), *Punica granatum* (pomegranate), and *Prunis dulcis* (almond)—their trunks painted white—are grown in planting spaces set in the courtyard floor. Ornamental climbers and/or fruit trees are trained against the walls. Instead of beds and borders there are plants in pots, which can be moved around to change the look of the garden. Seasonal variety is introduced by changing the containerized plants. The classic summer Mediterranean planting is scarlet *Pelargonium* (geraniums) in small terracotta pots, liberally distributed throughout the garden. Other popular potted ornamental species include *Helianthus* (sunflowers), *Mirabilis jalapa*, *Heliotropium arborescens*, and the climbers *Ipomoea purpurea* (morning

glory) and bougainvillea. Larger pots, planted with citrus, *Oleander*, the palm *Trachycarpus fortuneii*, and the blue-flowering bulb, *Agapanthus*, add height and ornament. To complete the atmosphere, there must be a profusion of fragrant herbs such as lavender, basil, oregano, and thyme.

The plan shows a white-walled courtyard divided into two areas by internal walls painted kingfisher blue, which echoes the color of the Greek flag. The floor is constructed from honey-yellow sandstone flags set at sufficient distance apart to allow grass or a scented herb such as thyme or chamomile to grow up between them. Next to the house, shaded by two olive trees, is an area for entertaining, where the distant sound of falling water can be heard.

Large ornate terracotta pots, evocative of Italy and planted with lemon trees, flank the doorway into the house. Lemon trees also flank a wrought-iron gate on the left-hand side of the garden (not visible on the plan). There is a mural painted on the wall of the gateway, which gives the illusion of looking out onto a Mediterranean scene. Passing between the blue walls, you enter the secluded area designed for relaxation. A wooden pergola clad with vines is a shady retreat from which to admire the water featire. It is of a plain, modern design in keeping with the garden's character, and is surrounded by a mass planting of lavender. A bougainvillea, *Ipomoea* (morning glory) and *Prunus dulcis* are trained against the walls, while pots of herbs and scarlet pelargonium are scattered throughout the courtyard.

White walls (below) are traditional in many countries where hot summers are guaranteed, as are plants that produce flowers in flamboyant colors.

Bright pelargoniums (bottom) are found everywhere in the Mediterranean and are particularly useful because they can withstand quite dry conditions. They are also excellent plants for containers and baskets.

tropical paradise

Enveloped by the verdant luxury of extraordinary foliage and contrasting bright flowers, cooled and calmed by the rush of cascading water, the "tame jungle" of a tropical courtyard is a place to reinvigorate the mind and spirit, whether in tropical or temperate areas.

To create a truly tropical courtyard garden you must either live in a region that enjoys a tropical climate, or cheat and cover your courtyard with a heated greeenhouse. Indeed, the 19th-century origins of the designed tropical garden began inside the huge hothouses built by the very wealthy in Europe and North America to display the extraordinary plants being brought back by plant hunters from the world's newly explored jungles. Built between 1836 and 1840, the great conservatory at Chatsworth, in Derbyshire, England, was the largest in the world. To maintain the correct temperature the heating system burned a ton of coal a day. Although initially the plants were exhibited individually, almost like museum pieces, it soon became fashionable to arrange the exciting introductions together, in a manner that imitated their natural environment. In this way, the "tame jungle" was born.

The tropical garden has once again become popular. In the past generation or so an international tropical garden style has developed in many ex-colonial countries, characterized by a fusion between art and nature. However, if you do not have a tropical climate, it is still possible to achieve a jungle-like effect in a temperate zone. Use the same principles, but plant half-hardy and hardy exotics instead of tender ones. There are hundreds of varieties from which to choose, including *Musa basjoo* (banana), *Chamaerops humilis* (dwarf fan palm), *Gunnera tinctoria*, and *Isoplexis canariensis*, all of which will give your garden that exotic, jungle-like quality.

The aim is to create a space that feels like a natural opening in a jungle—somewhere you want to stop, rest, and quench your thirst. Complementing the natural elements are the artistic, manufactured features. A path takes you to a seating area hidden among the rich foliage and protected against tropical rainstorms by a large umbrella—palm fronds supported on a wooden frame —or even a garden building such as a guesthouse. Other artistic adornments include water features, ornamental water jars, sculptures, and carvings, and religious iconography such as a statue of Buddha.

The planting arrangement is another area where the artistic hand is visible. It is dominated by bold, informal drifts of individual species of varying heights, which contrast with specimen plants positioned for visual impact. The planting must appear jungle-like and lush, particularly around the courtyard's perimeter, in order to disguise the courtyard's shape and create the impression that the space is larger than it actually is. A particularly effective technique is to attach pots planted with exotic orchids and bromeliads to the walls.

One of the delights of artistic tropical gardening is that there is an enormous variety of species available from all parts of the world, so there is no reason to restrict yourself to plants native to your country or region—unless, of course, that is what you want. Mixing and matching offers so much scope, and the effects can be as dramatic as they are colorful. However, remember that in a tropical climate many species grow very large very quickly. Therefore select your plants with care and tend towards using slow-growing and/or small species.

The "jungle space" shown on the plan overleaf has a tropical island feel, imparted by the path and the central patio. These are made from irregularly shaped but smoothed blocks of white stone (imitation coral), with the gaps between filled with black sand. The seating area is defined on one side by the informal pool, and on the other by the sinuous rill that flows from the millstone bubbler fountain. This gentle, serpentine watercourse is in contrast to the lively tumble of the naturalistic cascade which, constructed from large rocks, rises some 4ft above ground level.

A flavor of the tropics (below) is achieved with exotic plants that include palms, ferns, and bamboos. These provide a cool, lush background for other extravagant species with vivid flowers.

plants for a tropical courtyard

1 *Cyathea cooperi*

2 *Vanda tricolor*

3 Bromeliads in pots
  on the wall

4 *Anthurium andraeanum*

5 *Heliconia psittacorum*

6 *Tradescantia spathacea*

7 *Tabebuia aurea*

8 *Hedychium coronarium*

9 *Hypoestes phyllostachya*

10 *Impatiens platypetala*

11 *Aechmea fosteriana*

12 *Neoregelia carolinae*

13 *Stephanotis jasminoides*

14 *Impatiens hawkeri*

15 *Neoregelia ampullacea*

16 *Cordyline fruticosa*

17 *Pandanus pygmaeus*

18 *Strobilanthes dyeranus*

19 *Pachystachys lutea*

20 *Acalypha wilkesiana*
  'Godseffiana'

21 *Thunbergia erecta*

22 *Passiflora vitifolia*

23 *Pritchardia pacifica*

24 *Alocasia sanderiana*

25 *Strelitzia reginae*

26 *Nymphaea nouchali*
  var. *caerulea*

The change in level also creates a backdrop and effectively hides a corner that is awkwardly shaped.

The planting scheme embraces the concept of using species from different countries in bold swathes that form contrasts with the specimen plants. The pool is planted only with the beautiful blue-flowering water lily, *Nymphaea nouchali* var. *caerulea*, but you could create a carpet of color by adding other species, for example the bronze-red *N. ampla*, the yellow *N. stuhlmannii*, or the fragrant, white-flowering *N. pubescens*. Low-growing plants surrounding the pool and the seating area are used for ground cover, but toward the perimeter larger species blend with key, eye-catching specimens. These have been chosen to emphasize bold foliage, color and form, with flowering plants that have unusual and/or scented blooms, such as *Passiflora vitifolia* (passion flower) and *Hedychium coronarium* (ginger lily).

Black-and-white paving (above) gives a sense of structure and space to this courtyard. However, the rich planting, which includes cloud topiary, blurs the boundaries, creating a jungle-like atmosphere.

A temperate jungle (left) can be created using hardy plants that have exotic foliage and form, such as *Rheum palmatum*, *Gunnera manicata*, hostas, and bamboos. The aim is to create a dense and varied planting display, and to include water.

tropical paradise | **69**

easy-care options

There are many ways in which a garden can be made exciting and attractive without involving a good deal of work. The key to an easy-care garden is a framework of hard landscaping materials that are integrated with low-maintenance planting zones and features.

A first step in making your garden beautiful and easy to maintain would be to dispense with the lawn. Grass, contrary to popular mythology, is far from low maintenance. Even an average lawn requires weekly mowing in the growing period: a perfect lawn needs cutting almost daily. And then there is all the additional hard work—feeding, weeding, watering, raking, aerating, and so on.

Replace at least part of the area that was lawn with hard landscaping. Aim for variety within the framework—but be methodical. Carefully select a few materials and colors that work well together and complement other elements, such as the boundaries, the plants, or the features. For example, a patio could be colored concrete, paving slabs, or decking; a concealed seating area and pool could have a floor of brick or cobbles; while a path, which provides continuity and draws the framework together, could be colored gravel, crazy paving, or wood chips. Once in place, such hard surfaces require minimal care—killing the occasional weed that grows through the gaps.

The framework defines the planting zones, which in a courtyard also includes the vertical boundaries. Self-clinging climbers, such as variegated ivies and *Parthenocissus tricuspidata* (Boston ivy), can be used to cloak concrete, stone, or brick, and need little more than an annual pruning. Although all plants require a degree of maintenance, an effective way to minimize the workload is to plant mixed borders, in which shrubs and other tall species provide year-round structure. At a lower level, foliage and flowering perennials, ferns and bulbs weave together to create a dense covering of seasonal interest, and in so doing, help to suppress weed growth.

To further reduce maintenance, exchange most of the low-growing plants for hard surface materials such as gravel or shale. Scatter a good amount of fertilizer over the planting zone and cover with a

Low maintenance (left) need not mean uninteresting. Attractively curved walls define unusual garden spaces, while the exotic planting will require only a modicum of care.

Woven willow (opposite) is used to create raised beds, which have been filled with box plants. In no time this will make an organic display carpeted in green, which will only require an occasional trimming. The gravel will not need any care whatsoever.

membrane to prevent weeds from growing through the gravel and the gravel sinking into the soil. A woven polypropylene membrane, as used on nursery beds, is easier to install and secure than black polythene sheeting. It does not rip or fall apart, and allows water through to the plants' roots. Cover with 3in of gravel, put the plants in position and scrape back the gravel. Cut the membrane, pull it back, and plant, then replace both membrane and gravel.

Other crucial constituents of the easy-care courtyard are the features or focal points. These are a matter of personal taste, but in addition to sculpture, include water features, architectural plants, a few jagged rocks, or some large water-washed cobbles. A garden with a desert theme could feature multi-colored gravel.

The plan overleaf is of a green, meditative garden in which the features echo this reflective mood. As you leave the house, your eye focuses on the modern sculpture (also visible from within the

secluded seating area) and you hear the sound of falling water. Progressing along the path, the cascade becomes visible, with a mirror that reveals the secret garden hidden away in the center of the bed. This is a shady, mossy retreat with space for one person to sit. Further on is the arch marking the entrance to the secluded sitting area. Here the floor is cobbled and the enclosing bamboo screen has a bamboo roller blind that can be raised to offer a reverse view of the modern sculpture. Walking through a bamboo curtain, the secret path returns you to the house. Lighting is a strong theme, with the path lit throughout and the sculptures and ornaments illuminated to heighten their impact.

The planting uses taller plants chosen and positioned to achieve particular effects. Bamboo makes a wonderful thin hedge, as well as a frame for the sculpture. Certain species have a strong architectural form, while evergreen shrubs block views—a way of

INNISFIL PUBLIC LIBRARY

plants for an easy-care courtyard

1 *Wisteria sinensis* **2** *Erythronium americanum*
3 *Erythronium dens-canis* **4** *Hemerocallis citrina*
5 *Rosa glauca* **6** *Mahonia aquifolium*
7 *Colchicum autumnale* **8** *Daphne odora*
'Aureomarginata' **9** *Cordyline australis* 'Torbay
Dazzler' **10** *Parthenocissus henryana*
11 *Camellia saluenensis* **12** *Athyrium filix-femina*
13 *Narcissus pseudonarcissus*
14 *Crinodendron hookerianum*
15 *Trillium grandiflorum* **16** *Correa* 'Mannii'
17 *Asplenium scolopendrium* **18** *Chimonanthus
praecox* **19** *Cyclamen coum* **20** *Acer palmatum*
var. *dissectum* Dissectum Atropurpureum Group
21 *Rhododendron falconeri* **22** *Meconopsis
betonicifolia* **23** *Hosta fortunei* var.
aureomarginata **24** *Magnolia stellata*
25 *Trachycarpus fortunei* **26** *Phyllostachys
bambusoides* 'Allgold' **27** *Bergenia ciliata*
28 *Kniphofia caulescens* **29** *Cornus capitata*
30 *Convallaria majalis* **31** *Epimedium
perralderianum* **32** *Camellia japonica*
'Tricolor' **33** *Phyllostachys nigra*
34 *Abelia* x *grandiflora*
35 *Hosta* 'Halcyon'
36 *Cistus ladanifer*
37 *Rosa* 'Aloha'
38 *Matteuccia struthiopteris*
39 *Phormium* 'Dazzler'
40 *Garrya elliptica*
41 *Viburnum carlesii*
42 *Alchemilla mollis*
43 *Hamamelis mollis*
44 *Lilium regale*
45 *Cortaderia selloana*
46 *Dicksonia antarctica*

maintaining surprise, a feeling of mystery about what is around the corner. For dynamism and seasonal variety, deciduous shrubs with interesting foliage and/or good fall color are matched with flowering species, with fragrance from both.

The variety of lower-growing species included in the courtyard is diverse; it is designed to change with the seasons, although an alternative, to reduce maintenance, would be to plant large drifts of true ground cover species such as *Lamium maculatum* 'Beacon Silver' (dead nettle), *Rubus tricolor*, or *Gaultheria procumbens*. Many climbers, such as clematis and honeysuckle, roses and wisteria, can also be laid flat and grown as ground cover, and although they will not grow thick enough to prevent weeds, they do look striking when planted in this way.

Dense plantings (above) of shrubs and herbaceous species effectively suppress weed growth and reduce the time spent weeding. Even in a shady garden, there are many species that will thrive in a minimal light setting, and fill the available space with interesting textures and shapes.

The hard landscaping (below) of the paving provides a low maintenance surface, particularly in comparison to an area of grass. The color of the slabs perfectly complements that of the planting, thereby introducing overall unity, while the flat, simple lines contrast with the exuberance of the foliage.

romantic senses

The romantic courtyard appeals to the emotions as well as to the senses. It is an intensely personal garden, a place to cocoon yourself away from the world in a space that fills you with ease and contentment.

Misty shades (top) of pink and white surround a secluded seat, which provides a view over a pool. The simple lines of the wooden decking and its organic texture and color add to the sense of calm.

An archway smothered with clematis (above) gives a glimpse of a verdant retreat on the other side of the wall. The trick with romantic planting is to make use of gentle forms and subtle colors.

A safe haven (opposite) hidden away from the world is the ideal place for romance. At night the large brass lanterns provide soft light; for increased privacy the structure could be roofed over or covered with climbers.

A romantic courtyard is best summed up by the word sanctuary. We all need time to get away from those things that trouble us, and a secret garden with features and plants that create an atmosphere of tranquillity and repose provides an escape—a perfect haven in which to be alone or spend time with those we love. Privacy and seclusion are essential to generate that feeling of being cocooned. A romantic courtyard must therefore be well hidden from neighbors and contain small, intimate areas, as well as spaces in which to entertain when you are feeling more congenial.

Tall boundaries block out the external world, and panels of trellis work attached to the top of fences or walls and covered with climbers are effective screens. To avoid being overlooked, you also need some form of overhead structure. Free-standing buildings such as summerhouses are attractive features in their own right, but for something less solid, a pergola covered with scented climbers offers seclusion, fragrance, and dappled shade. More exotic are metal-framed structures covered with brightly colored fabrics; the frames can be made into all sorts of shapes, such as a crusader's tent or a sail-like shelter. Living structures can be made by weaving sapling trees together to form a verdant arbor or a bower.

Comfortable seating or cushions scattered on the (dry) floor will make the secluded spot more romantic, while music and soft candlelight will gently stimulate the senses. However, do not forget that plants, too, can be romantic. Green is a restful color and a foliage backdrop is soothing to the eye, while color and perfume from flowers can be very evocative. It is important to include winter and early sping flowering species such as *Hamamelis* (witch hazel), *Mahonia*, or *Viburnum*, as they will draw you outside on mild days and will raise your spirits when viewed from the house. To complete the scene, there should be the sight and/or sound of gently flowing water. And you can add to the garden's romantic appeal by including your own personal associations or passions—a reminder, perhaps, of where you and your partner met, or of plants that you associate with loved ones, or memories of a wonderful holiday.

The plan overleaf for a romantic courtyard combines romance and seclusion with year-round planting and spaces for being sociable. The paved area near the house (at the top of the plan) is large

enough for a table and chairs, but behind the climber-covered trellis there is a private nook for one or two people. The *chaise-longue* (there is space for two) is hidden away, surrounded by potted plants. The beds are planted to create interest during the four seasons, and as well as having interesting forms, many of them also have fragrant flowers. And while you are relaxing you can hear the tinkling sound of falling water in the distance.

The backdrop to the beds is a dark green hedge of yew, through which scrambles the vividly colored, scarlet-flowered climber *Tropaeolum speciosum* (flame creeper). A series of arches, dripping with both the blue and white forms of the richly perfumed wisteria, lead to the archway in the hedge. On the ground, gravel takes the place of paving, signalling a transition from one area of the garden to another. A third arch, which is hung with the heavily scented *Trachelospermum asiaticum* (star jasmine), leads to an old-fashioned kissing gate, which marks the entrance to the sanctuary.

The paving returns and provides continuity, but this is an even more private space. The leafy willow bower, through which rambles sweet-smelling jasmine, is a hideaway. The bower roof and sides frame the view of the garden—in particular the raised bed and the classical statue of Hercules, which matches the one of the goddess Flora in the front garden. The raised bed has a natural feel, and the rocks add further height and texture. In winter

they stand like sentinels, and in summer they rise up from the green carpet of hosta species and ferns. The curvaceous water feature contrasts with the angularity of the rocks. Water movement adds dynamism, and because the rate of flow is relatively slow, it mesmerizes, while the sound is calming and peaceful.

The overall planting, as elsewhere, is for four-season effect, with a strong emphasis on fragrance. The shrubs provide structure, and *Hamamelis mollis* winter and early spring interest, while the *Rhododendron luteum* (a yellow azalea) and *Convallaria majalis* (lily-of-the-valley) have scented flowers in spring. In the back bed the emphasis is on yellow, scented flowers, which in summer bring a dash of color to contrast with the green ferns, and provide a backdrop to the area as a whole.

This comely maiden (top) is the perfect statue for emphasizing the romantic aspects of a courtyard garden. Surrounded by fragrant roses, she is the epitome of grace and repose, and hints at the enduring nature of love.

Japanese anemone (center), *Anemone* x *hybrida,* is an example of the type of plant particularly suitable for a romantic garden. It is available in a range of colors and hues, from white through pink to wine-red. The flowers have the requisite look for this style of courtyard—elegant but not showy.

A sense of time (left) is captured in the elegance of this weathered and lichen-encrusted horse's head. As with the statue of the young woman, it is a fine example of how classical themes can work well in a romantic courtyard setting.

plants for a romantic courtyard

1 *Campsis radicans*

2 *Rosa* 'Maigold'

3 *Clematis montana*

4 *Cytisus battandieri*

5 *Lavandula stoechas*

6 *Canna indica* (red)

7 *Yucca whipplei*

8 *Dianthus* 'Musgrave's Pink'

9 *Lonicera periclymenum*
'Graham Thomas'

10 *Clematis armandii*

11 *Thymus vulgaris*

12 *Stauntonia hexaphylla*

13 *Buddleja davidii* 'Black Knight'

14 *Anemone* x *hybrida* (pink)

15 *Cotinus coggygria* 'Notcutt's
Variety'

16 *Delphinium* 'Mighty Tom'

17 *Rhododendron yakushimanum*
'Koichiro Wada'

18 *Dianthus* 'Haytor White'

19 *Daphne mezereum*

20 *Digitalis* x *mertonensis*

21 *Trachelospermum asiaticum*

22 *Wisteria floribunda*

23 *Wisteria floribunda* 'Alba'

24 *Lilium regale*

25 *Philadelphus* 'Erectus'

26 *Geranium renardii*

27 *Cistus* x *cyprius*

28 *Hyacinthoides non-scriptus*

29 *Hamamelis mollis*

30 *Taxus baccata*

31 *Tropaeolum speciosum*

32 *Jasminum officinale*

33 *Jasminum officinale* 'Aureum'

34 *Rosa* 'Indigo'

35 *Hemerocallis lilioasphodelus*

36 *Inula hookeri*

37 *Carpenteria californica*

38 *Hosta* 'Halcyon'

39 *Asplenium scolopendrium*

40 *Matteuccia struthiopteris*

41 *Dicksonia antarctica*

42 *Dryopteris filix-mas*

43 *Hosta undulata* var.
albomarginata

44 *Hosta sieboldii*

45 *Rhododendron luteum*

edible bounty

An edible garden has an edge over a purely ornamental garden; it not only produces crops, but also provides a constantly changing display—one that is every bit as attractive as a garden overflowing with shrubs and flowers.

Edible gardening brings the joy of picking sun-warm tomatoes from the vine or unearthing the first new potatoes, a feeling matched only by the enjoyment of eating produce fresh from the garden. Another of the great delights is the wide choice of fruit, vegetables, and herbs that can be grown, with the result that you can experiment each new season with different crops and recipes. Growing your own also puts you in charge—you can select non-genetically modified seed, grow the older, tastier varieties, and garden organically. And on top of all this, edible gardening is one of the best ways to bring gardening and cooking to children, for they become completely engrossed in the whole production process, from seed to salsa.

The most obvious way to create an edible garden is to dedicate the whole area to the production of crops. It was the French who first fully realized this possibility in the 16th century when they devised the potager. Literally a "kitchen garden," the word potager has come to mean an ornamental vegetable garden. Perhaps the finest example is at Villandry, on the banks of the Loire, France, where, within nine squares defined by an elaborate system of low box hedges and gravel walks, is an extraordinary patchwork of colorful vegetables, aromatic herbs, espaliered fruit, and bright flowers.

Villandry is a large garden, but the concept of the formal potager layout can easily be transferred to the courtyard. However, this is not the only way in which you can design an edible courtyard. You can turn to the monastic gardens of medieval Europe for inspiration, and use raised beds. These are features in their own right, and an effective way of demarcating the garden. They can be made from wood, woven willow, brick, or painted concrete blocks in a range of different shapes, although rectangular or square are the easiest kind to make. Alternatively, beds can be at ground level and enclosed by small hedges or low fences, or simply demarcated by paths. Paths are best made from a hard surface in order to minimize soil compaction in winter and for ease in maneuvering a wheelbarrow.

Planting styles offer even more scope for variety. Regimented rows of different crops within a bed look neat and ordered, especially if there is variety in height and foliage type. Planting in blocks gives a tapestry effect, while crops grown in clumps or drifts are informal.

At first glance (right), what appears to be a shrub and flower garden is, on closer examination, a garden largely of herbs, vegetables, and fruit—demonstrating that the edible can also be beautiful.

There is no need to use the whole courtyard for crops in order to reap their ornamental rewards. Mixing fruit and vegetables with ornamental species can be as spectacular as it is unusual. Begin by training fruit trees into different shapes against the walls, making certain that nectarine, fig, and peach are against a warm, sunny boundary. You can also make delightful wall coverings from scramblers such as blackberries or vines. In beds and borders, fruit bushes make excellent feature plants, while the scarlet flowers and fresh green foliage of runner beans make a wonderful backdrop or a temporary hedge. Herbs will fit in anywhere. The roundness of cabbages, the crinkly red leaves of lollo rossa, and fluffy foliage of carrots add different textures to a flowerbed. *Solanaceae*—tomatoes (red, green, and yellow), peppers, chilies, eggplant —all add color.

The graceful *Cynara cardunculus* (cardoon), a relative of the artichoke, has exotic foliage and electric blue flowers, and makes a splash in any herbaceous border. Many cucurbits—gourds, squashes, zucchini, and so on—with striking leaves, bright flowers, and unusual fruit, can be used as exotic ground cover or as a display grown over a support. On the smallest scale, a hanging basket planted with herbs or trailing tomatoes can be added to an ornamental garden.

The plan overleaf combines beauty with utility—a formal ornamental layout full of crops. Around the walls, whitewashed to reflect light and heat into the garden, fruit trees are trained as fans, espaliers, and cordons, shapes that are pieces of art. The small circular beds near the house are dedicated to soft fruit trees (blackcurrant and gooseberry) and strawberries; they flank a space for a table and chairs, where you can sit alfresco and admire your hard work or eat its results. The matching beds at the other end of the garden are planted with summer salad crops. In the winter and spring, these could be planted with seasonal bedding to fill the bare soil and add a dash of color. This plan is not a blueprint, and these beds could be planted with different crops, or even perhaps flowers for cutting, with *Lathyrus odorata* (sweet pea) replacing the runner beans and cucumber on the ornamental tepee frames.

The central circle, with its raised beds and maze pattern paving slab, is designed to look interesting. The posts and ropes add height and structure, and could be planted with climbers such as climbing roses, jasmine, clematis, or honeysuckle, or fruit crops such as blackberry or loganberry, or a mixture of both. The four quarters are devoted to vegetables and herbs. They are of an easy size to maintain, but there is a practical reason for four beds. Growing the same crops in the same place year after year can cause nutrition deficiencies and a build-up of pests and diseases. To minimize problems, a four-year crop rotation program is used. Each bed is planted with a single crop group, and at the end of each growing season the crops are moved one bed to the left (or right.) This means that at the start of the fifth season you are back where you began. The table below lists the four crop groups with a few examples.

The foliage montage (above) of several brassicas is a study in exciting and exotic shapes, textures, and colors. The frothy leaves and white flowers of *Cosmos* help to lighten the display.

Mixing and matching (opposite) creates an unusual design. The ironwork pillars are covered with scarlet runner beans and sweet peas, which blend perfectly with the underplanted begonias and strawberries.

Herbs (below), irrespective of their planting arrangements and associations, never fail to look attractive—especially when combined with ornamental perennials.

Legumes & Pods	Alliums	Solanaceous	Brassicas
Broad beans, French and runner beans, lima beans, dolchas beans, peanuts, peas, okra	Bulb onions, green onions, shallots, leeks, garlic, European onions, Welsh onions	Tomatoes, sweet peppers, eggplant, celery, celeriac	Bok choy, cauliflower, cabbage, Brussels sprouts, broccoli, kohl-rabi, Chinese cabbage

plants for an edible courtyard

1 Peach (*Prunus persica*) **2** Fig (*Ficus carica*)

3 Red runner bean (*Phaseolus coccineus*)

4 Cucumber (*Cucumis sativus*) **5** Pear (*Pyrus communis*) **6** Lettuce (*Lactuca sativa*) 'Cos'

7 Lettuce (*Lactuca sativa*) 'Lollo Rosso'

8 Lettuce (*Lactuca sativa*) 'Butterhead'

9 Spinach (*Spinacia oleracea*) **10** Salad rocket (*Eruca vesicaria*) **11** Tomato (*Lycopersicon esculentum*) **12** Radish (*Raphanus sativus*)

13 Bulb and green onion (*Allium cepa*) **14** Apricot (*Prunus armeniaca*) **15** Apple (*Malus domestica*)

16 Parsnip (*Pastinaca sativa*) **17** Carrot (*Daucus carota*) **18** Potato (*Solanum tuberosum*) **19** Basil (*Ocimum basilicum*) **20** Greek oregano (*Origanum vulgare* ssp. *hirtum*) **21** Turnip (*Brassica rapa* Rapifera Group) **22** Brussels sprout (*Brassica oleracea* Gemmifera Group) **23** Cabbage (*Brassica oleracea* Capitata Group) **24** Parsley (*Petroselinum crispum*) **25** Garden thyme (*Thymus vulgaris*)

26 Broad bean (*Vicia faba*) **27** Pea (*Pisum sativum*)

28 French bean (*Phaseolus vulgaris*)

29 Peppermint (*Mentha* x *piperita*) **30** Dill (*Anethum graveolens*) **31** Plum (*Prunus domestica*)

32 Garlic (*Allium sativum*) **33** Leek (*Allium porrum*)

34 Coriander (*Coriandrum sativum*) **35** Marjoram (*Origanum majorana*) **36** Strawberry (*Fragaria* x *ananassa*) **37** Blackcurrant (*Ribes nigrum*)

38 Gooseberry (*Ribes uva-crispa*)

This courtyard will provide a wide range of fruit and vegetables in season, but if you want early crops, you may want to make space for a greenhouse and/or a cold frame, sited in a sunny spot. However, regardless of whether you plant your whole garden with food crops, or just integrate a few plants into your existing garden, the scope for inventive and attractive gardening with edible crops is enormous. Whatever you grow will bring satisfaction and achievement when you sit down to eat your home-grown produce— and, perhaps satisfaction knowing you have also saved yourself money; home grown is cheaper than the supermarket.

This formal herb garden (top left) has a hint of the knot garden about it, and imparts a Renaissance feel, emphasized by the old cauldrons used as pots. In addition to being very pretty, the bed is low maintenance, because there is no bare soil in which weeds could get a foothold.

The decaying wall (left), with its unusual texture and color, is a striking backdrop for this harmonious display of herbs. The carpeting mounds of thyme species, the purple sage, and the upright angelica all stand apart, yet blend together in perfect harmony.

entertaining ideas

A courtyard that provides space for entertaining is two gardens in one—a place in which to enjoy a meal with family and friends, and a quiet garden to delight in on your own once everyone has left. With careful planning, taking into consideration the comfort of your guests as well as your own, you will be able to create a garden that adequately fulfills these conditions.

A place for alfresco entertaining is a room outside, comprising walls, a floor, furniture, and decoration, where the ceiling is the sky. Successful entertaining requires the right ambience—a welcoming atmosphere in a comfortable space. Consider the way in which people and objects interact, and work out how much space each feature needs in relation to the average person. As in your dining room, for example, a chair at a table needs enough space around it to be pulled out, and you have to be able to move around it and sit down without bumping into your neighbor.

Scented plants, soft lighting and music, and comfortable seating—whether wooden chairs, wrought iron seats, stone benches, or just rugs and cushions scattered on the ground—set the mood for relaxed entertaining. And if you wish to eat outside, the table can be a decorative feature in its own right—or a more simple, portable, one that can be folded up and stored when not in use.

For comfort, awnings, umbrellas, canopies, or trees will protect guests from harsh sun and rain. Lighting is another essential and, for subtle effects, candles are a good option, especially those that repel insects. If you are hardy and want to be outside in cooler

Friendly and welcoming (right), this sheltered dining area is a place in which visitors will instinctively feel at home. The table is positioned to take advantage of the view, while the aquamarine pool is as enticing as it is cool.

Protected from the heat of the sun (below) by the tiled roof, wooden benches furnished with soft cushions offer a place to sit, relax, and entertain guests. The serving-counter-cum-bar in the corner is a particularly civilized addition, avoiding the need to keep returning to the house for provisions.

A double avenue of trees (right) defines the dining area and provides a shady canopy of foliage. The garden feels much larger because of the cunning use of a mirror, placed to face the table—which is an imposing feature in its own right.

A profusion of exotic foliage (opposite right) encloses a secret hideaway in which to enjoy al fresco meals. The wooden furniture, simple but attractive, has weathered gently so that it matches the wooden decking that elevates the area.

A scattering of vibrant colored cushions (left) and a bright painted wall provide striking contrasts to the more subdued colors of cane and wood. There is more than a hint of the tropics in this courtyard design, which is suitably enhanced by the bold architectural planting.

A small corner (above) provides an intimate setting for an outdoor dining room. The backdrop of deep green ivy is the perfect foil for the black wrought-iron furniture, while the wall light and candles make dining after dark a possibility.

Texture and pattern (opposite) make a considerable contribution to the elegant formality of this courtyard garden (seen also on page 9). Glass tabletops not only increase the amount of available light, but also provide reflective surfaces that mingle the brickwork beneath with the greenery with the sky overhead.

weather, you may want to install a small heater. Space is often at a premium, so features for entertaining may need to play a dual role. A functional concrete seat could also be a piece of art; a marble table could be a stand for potted plants as well as a place for serving food; built-in seats can have hinged lids for storage; and herbs are ornamental and provide fragrance as well as being edible.

The plants, while beautiful in their own right, can also serve as a welcoming feature. Those near the seating and dining areas should preferably have strongly perfumed flowers, but choose species that bloom when you are using the garden most—perhaps fragrant roses in the summer, or in a hot climate, in the evening, *Matthiola longipetala* (night-scented stock), or the deliciously scented *Nicotiana* (tobacco plant). Unusual plants can be used as a lure and, when placed at a distance, will be an invitation to explore other areas of the courtyard.

The plan shows a courtyard that has been designed for a range of entertaining activities. Immediately outside the door into the garden is the cooking and dining area, and away to the left is an area of lawn for relaxation. To unify the two areas and help instill a calm atmosphere, the walls are painted a soft rose pink.

The color theme of the flowers is white, soft blue, red, and pink, with the occasional eye-catcher such as *Potentilla fruticosa* 'Red Ace', *Taxus baccata* 'Fastigiata', and *Cornus florida*. Many of the species also have scented flowers or foliage, such as *Lavandula* (lavender), which you brush past when leaving or entering the house, and *Rosa* 'Indigo'. The rose-pink theme is picked up in the dining area. The table is surrounded by a ring of pink granite paving slabs with radiating spokes that lead to four pink granite pots planted with herbs. The other two colors are repeated in the white granite paving slabs of the floor, and in the dazzling white bark of the four birch trees—*Betula utilis* var. *jacquemontii* 'Silver Shadow'—shading the dining table during the day and provide a leafy canopy through which the stars twinkle at night. A thick glass table, which appears ice blue, provides the focal point in the dining area.

To complete the color matching and unify the garden, one of the twin arched bowers at either end of the garden is covered in white wisteria and surrounded with white lavender; the other is blue. The cooking station against the far wall features a barbecue and a beehive terracotta oven with workspace. Once the entertaining is over, all the paraphernalia—the collapsible chairs, the cushions, the rugs and cooking equipment—can be stored out of the way in the dry wooden boxes placed beneath the seats in the arches.

plants for an entertaining courtyard

1 *Taxus baccata* 'Fastigiata'

2 *Iris* 'Carnaby' **3** *Iris* 'Early Light'

4 *Iris* 'Flamenco' **5** *Iris* 'Stepping Out'

6 *Rosa* 'Coral Dawn'

7 *Monarda* 'Croftway Pink'

8 *Potentilla fruticosa* 'Red Ace'

9 *Hemerocallis* 'Stafford'

10 *Laurus nobilis*

11 *Origanum vulgare*

12 *Betula utilis* var. *jacquemontii* 'Silver Shadow'

13 *Ocimum basilicum*

14 *Rosa gallica* var. *officinalis* 'Versicolor'

15 *Nicotiana alata*

16 *Lavandula angustifolia* 'Alba'

17 *Wisteria sinensis* 'Alba'

18 *Cornus florida*

19 *Convolvulus tricolor*

20 *Allium schoenoprasum*

21 *Thymus vulgaris*

22 *Lavandula angustifolia*

23 *Nepeta* x *faassenii*

24 *Rosa* 'Indigo'

25 *Delphinium* 'Blue Nile'

26 *Lilium regale*

27 *Wisteria sinensis*

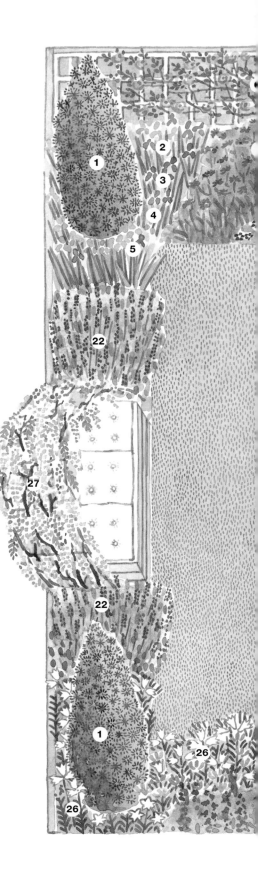

the spa
treatment

The spa garden is dedicated to relaxing and entertaining. It is a place to enjoy a range of pleasurable and health-giving treatments within an attractive garden framework that can be tailored to suit all tastes and climates. With careful planning, the courtyard will successfully marry the practical with the decorative.

The spa courtyard can be created and enjoyed anywhere—a night-time soak in the bubbling warmth of a hot tub when the ground is covered in snow is as pleasant as a midday, post-sauna cold plunge when it is 100°F in the shade. It is a very congenial style, as it encourages friends, neighbors. and family to drop by, enjoy the spa, chat, and unwind. And because planting can be kept to a minimum, this courtyard requires little maintenance.

Treatments—sauna, hot tub, steam room, cold plunge pool, and shower, dominate the spa courtyard, but it is also a garden. Therefore, your design needs to be dual purpose: Decide on the treatments you want to enjoy and on the style of garden within which you wish to arrange them. This offers great freedom of choice, as spa treatments will meld easily with many garden styles. Where winters are cold, a Scandinavian atmosphere is appropriate: white-painted walls, wooden decking floors (from an environmentally sustainable source), sheltered corners, and

architectural planting will combine to create a traditional feel. For a Japanese flavor, line the walls with bamboo screens and make a small Zen rock and gravel garden, an approach that will also work well in areas with little rain. For a modern ambience, dyed concrete floors, mirrors on the walls, and stainless steel planters make an impact; and if you want a more informal, floral garden, simply set the treatment centers among flowerbeds and lawn. However, to minimize the amount of dirt getting into the various treatment centers, avoid the necessity of walking on loose flooring materials such as sand, gravel, or bark chips.

Once you have decided on treatments and style, the next stage is to integrate the two elements. Practicality is essential; the treatment centers should be easily accessible from the house and from each

A bubbling hot tub (opposite left), hidden away among exotic foliage, is as alluring on a warm summer's day as on a cold winter's evening.

Ornamental grasses (left) have been thoughtfully planted to provide an attractive living screen, which ensures privacy for the pool area and bathers.

The electric blue (above) of this plunge pool contrasts strongly but effectively with the terracotta tile floor. The asymmetric shape of the pool successfully breaks up the rectangular shape of the courtyard, while the planting blurs the edges. Both techniques help make the space feel larger than it is.

other. However, rather than being crowded together, they should be arranged in such a way that there are usable spaces between them. These spaces then become home to the screened-off, secluded areas for sitting and cooling off, open areas for entertaining, the beds/borders, and ornamental garden features, such as sculpture. As the courtyard will be used at night, the final task is to position the lights for easy movement around the garden as well as dramatic effect.

Beds provide a setting for the treatment centers and, if planted with sufficiently large plants, create visual blocks, thereby separating the courtyard into a series of experiences and increasing intimacy. To enjoy maximum relaxation and minimal maintenance, use a mixed planting of shrubs, herbaceous species, and bulbs. To keep matters even less labor intensive, plant architectural specimen shrubs such as *Corylus avellana* 'Contorta', *Salix babylonica* 'Tortuosa', or *Fremontodendron californicum* set within ground cover plants or a mulch of gravel or stone chips. If you have decided on a plunge pool, why not enhance borders of it with a bog garden planted with marginals such as candelabra *Primula* species, hosta, *Fillipendula*, and the spectacular *Zantedeschia aethiopica*. To prevent soil escaping into the pool, ensure that the bed is self-contained. To add another low-maintenance, artistic dimension, augment the beds with specimen plants in planters or large pots, and remember that, regardless of the effect you decide on, plants look fantastic at night if carefully lit.

The plan shows a design influenced by Scandinavian traditions and planted primarily with Chinese and Japanese architectural, evergreen specimen shrubs. The perimeter boundary is a white-painted fence, and wood and white dominate the courtyard. Near the house is the wooden decking seating-cum-entertaining area. The decking is raised 6in above ground level to allow drainage and air circulation; below the decking the ground is concrete or soil, with a permeable polypropylene membrane to suppress weeds. The flat decking is sheltered by the uplit *Betula populifolia* (gray birch) and an awning, which can be extended for increased privacy.

White granite rocks, a bed of marginal plants, and stainless steel planters soften the decking and introduce height. Moving forward, the asymmetrical plunge pool divides the garden, while the narrowing decking draws you through the gateway created by container-grown mahonia into the farther half of the garden.

In this half of the garden, surrounded by plants and accessed by decking stepping stones set in white granite chips, are the sauna (constructed from a large redwood barrel), and the hot tub, reached by climbing up two steps to the decking surround. The mixture of evergreen shrubs and ground cover, many of which flower and introduce seasonal variety, are features in their own right, but they also help to soften the layout and separate the treatment areas, creating the feeling that the garden is larger than it is.

plants for a spa courtyard

1 *Viola odorata*

2 *Tradescantia virginiana* (white)

3 *Magnolia stellata*

4 *Euonymus fortunei* 'Emerald 'n' Gold'

5 *Chaenomeles japonica*

6 *Phyllostachys bambusoide* 'Allgold'

7 *Prunus subhirtella* 'Autumnalis'

8 *Camellia* x *williamsii* 'Donation'

9 *Hamamelis mollis*

10 *Mahonia aquifolium* 'Apollo'

11 *Phyllostachys nigra* var. *henonis*

12 *Pinus mugo*

13 *Pleioblastus variegatus*

14 *Convallaria majalis*

15 *Euonymus fortuneii* 'Silver Queen'

16 *Chaenomeles speciosa*

17 *Mahonia japonica*

18 *Hakonechloa macra* 'Aureola'

19 *Betula populifolia*

20 *Phormium tenax* Purpureum Group

21 *Rubus tricolor*

22 *Dicksonia antarctica*

23 *Primula vialii*

24 *Hosta ventricosa*

25 *Matteuccia struthiopteris*

The angular shape of the pool (left) is defined by stone paving, which beautifully complements the blue tiles. There is a feeling of movement and vigor in this design.

Wooden decking (far left), the wooden dividing wall, and the raised wooden hot tub give this balcony garden a very organic look. This is picked up and emphasized by the earthenware pots, stone edging, and the architectural planting. The position of the hot tub allows views over the steel and glass boundary.

the
framework

boundaries

A courtyard is an enclosed and private space; its shape and vertical dimensions are defined by the perimeter boundaries. A variety of materials can be used to create this permanent structure, and because boundaries are so central to a courtyard they must be considered the first step in the design.

Stainless steel (above) provides an unusual but striking form of enclosure, which could be painted. The trellis panels are essential if plants are to be grown against the wall, as in extreme temperatures the metal could become either too hot or too cold, damaging any plants that touch it.

If you are starting with a blank canvas, the theme of the new garden should dictate the style of the boundary: For example, adobe walls for an arid courtyard, solid fencing for a Scandinavian spa, or corrugated iron for a design that looks to the future. Alternatively, if you are not taking a prescribed approach, such as a romantic or classical courtyard, choose materials that are in keeping with the house and that help to unify the two, or those that are indigenous to the area, such as the local stone or wood. If you are creating a new garden, but already have a boundary, you can adapt it to fit your style by painting walls and fences, creating openings to views beyond the garden and by growing plants to cover vertical surfaces.

The courtyard framework may also include vertical screens that divide it into smaller compartments or rooms. The selection criteria for these are the same as those for the boundaries: the material should match the theme. Yew hedges, for example, give an Arts and Crafts feel, while bamboo screens are appropriate for a Japanese courtyard. There are many modern materials that can be adapted to give a contemporary feel, and the planting scheme can be designed so that shrubs, bamboo and other specimens grow into a living screen (see page 104).

Where you have boundaries and a divided internal framework you also require entranceways and some means of linking the compartments. Gateways in the perimeter are a feature that not only provide access but may also frame a view of the landscape beyond your private world. Within the courtyard the screens can be pierced by features such as arches, tunnels, pergolas, and alleys, encouraging movement through the garden and adding interest and variety to the framework.

The sinuous wall (right) within this Mediterranean-style courtyard will cast eye-catching shadows. It also contrasts most effectively with the architectural form of the yuccas. A similarly curved perimeter hedge could be created with judicious planting and trimming.

Common building materials (opposite) such as scaffold poles and corrugated iron sheets are inexpensive, and can be converted into brightly colored internal partitions, which can be used to divide the garden into a series of compartments. Boundaries can also be used as vertical surfaces on which to display ornaments, pots, or works of art—in this case, sculpted metal lizards.

walls

Walls are the most permanent and solid materials with which to delineate your courtyard. Whether brick, concrete blocks, natural stone, slate, adobe, lava, or reinforced ferroconcrete, the choice depends on your garden style and budget, for walls require solid foundations, are expensive to build, and should be erected by a professional.

Recycling (above) pieces of glazed tile and broken chinaware creates a riot of color and texture. This informal mosaic is easy to achieve. The shards are set into mortar, which is applied to the wall, and can be shaped to create an undulating surface. However, it is advisable to plan the pattern before executing the scheme. Here the designer has included abstract shapes as well as flower and foliage forms. The same technique could also be used to great effect to make the lining of an ornamental pool.

When well built, walls require little maintenance and have many advantages. They absorb heat from the sun and radiate it back into the courtyard once the sun has set, keeping it warmer than would a wooden fence or hedge. Their sturdiness makes them a very effective sound insulator and a perfect support for structures such as pergolas, awnings, and trained plants.

Their vertical surface can be decorated with painted murals (such as that in the classical courtyard), mosaics, water features, and lights, while the brick bond or pattern in which the bricks are laid, and the mortar in which they are set, are an intrinsic decoration. The tops of walls may be coped, set with pots, or lined with trellis panels for additional height and privacy.

Internal walls may divide the courtyard, as in a Mediterranean garden, or form retaining walls where there is a change in level, as does a drystone wall in an Arts and Crafts garden. However, in windy locations walls can cause vortices, which may damage plants. In such circumstances, you will be better off using a porous perimeter such as a hedge (see page 104).

Picture this (above): Walls may be used very effectively to produce a visual block and divide a garden into compartments. In this case the hole in the wall acts as a picture frame for a modern sculpture, but it could as well define a vista away from the garden into the landscape beyond.

Ram's-head fountains (left) and attractive arching brick steps set into a wall are a key element of the garden layout. Painted planters and cones of ivy add to the structure, while the plants in the beds at top and bottom of the wall soften its edges.

A gateway can be turned into an ornamental aperture, and while a solid wooden gate creates the feeling of a definite end to the garden, a wrought-iron gate can form a frame for the landscape beyond. If there is no view, a solid gate will give the impression that your garden is much bigger, suggesting the existence of another, secret garden that lies beyond the one you are in. And a see-through gate placed in front of a mural depicting a view that is in keeping with the garden's theme—for example, a distant view of Mount Fuji in a Japanese garden—is pure illusion.

This is lighthearted fun (left), particularly if you have children. The brightly colored metal wall with animal shapes cut into it is exactly the type of lateral approach to the garden's structural elements that will give your courtyard individuality and character.

Changes in level (right) and the repeat planting of domes of box are the key to bringing this courtyard space to life. The continuity created by the extensive use of brick for steps and the walls of the raised beds ties the whole design together.

A plain and simple wall (below) brings purity to the courtyard space, and in this case makes it feel light and airy. The wall also serves as a screen against which the form and color of individual plants can be exhibited at their best.

fences and trellises

For enclosing a courtyard and dividing the spaces within, fences are inexpensive, instant, and easy to install. Wooden fencing comes in many different styles, but is essentially of two types, solid and open.

Solid fences provide privacy. They are constructed by attaching prefabricated panels between wooden or concrete posts. For a more imposing, solid fence, use rustic poles (preferably 8ft tall and 4-6in in diameter) set on end and side by side. You can vary the pole length to create a repeating pattern or an irregular, sawtooth effect. The appropriate height for a solid perimeter fence is 6ft, with an optional 2ft of trellis panels on top.

Just trellis (above) painted white or pale green, and minus plant cover, can transform a plain boundary by introducing texture and giving depth to an otherwise flat surface. The window mirror is a touch of fun, framed as it is by the potted palms on pedestals.

Imposing fencing (right), which in other circumstances could feel claustrophobic, is made a feature by adding the overhead spars to create a long pergola walk that has a cloistered look. The fresh green leaves and light gravel nicely counterbalance the dark wood. The water-washed cobbles add a neat touch.

The trellis framework (far right) is unusual, in that it stands away from the wall, with the plants planted behind it. This arrangement means that when fully grown, the plants will create a thick green wall supported by the trellis, adding an extra dimension to the rear of the house.

Twin cherubs (left) gaze down from the posts on either side of the pedestal. The posts emphasize the climber-clad trellis, while the green and white theme is picked up by the exotic foliage of the *Gunnera* and hosta, and the flowers of the iris, climbing rose, and *Zantedeschia*.

Woven willow panels (below) make a very organic, attractive form of screening, either as a perimeter fence, or as a way to divide the garden into compartments. Painting the posts is an effective method of breaking up the line of fencing and introducing a splash of color.

Open fences, such as picket or post-and-rail, allow views in and out, and are made from horizontal spars attached to uprights. This style is most attractive when less than 4ft in height, and should be used only where seclusion is not essential.

All fence posts should be anchored 18in into the ground with concrete, but in order to prevent rotting, wooden posts can be supported on concrete-in-metal brackets. For the same reason, always buy pressure-treated lumber and rest the fence panels on gravel boards. Alternatively, you can leave a 2in gap at the base. If you take these precautions and treat the wood with an annual coat of wood preservative or paint (be careful not to splash any plants), a wooden fence should last for 20 years.

Perimeter fences can also be made from cast iron railings, woven willow. and hazel panels, slivers of slate wired together, or even toughened, opaque or clear glass. These materials may also be used to divide the courtyard into compartments, as can wooden trellis panels, which are too flimsy for a perimeter. Covered with climbers, trellis panels are sufficiently open to give a hint of what is to come. Trellises may also be fixed to walls or made into tunnels. Traditional patterns are diamonds or squares, but some designs create optical illusions, making a small space seem much larger. However, if you want something unusual, make your own trellis, using, for example, copper tubing uprights linked horizontally by fishing line or, for a Japanese design, bamboo canes and dried heather screens.

hedges and living screens

A carefully maintained perimeter hedge provides security and privacy, and reduces the damage to plants in windy areas. Hedges are less expensive than a wall or fence, but they take time to establish and require regular clipping during the growing season.

An evergreen hedge, such as *Taxus baccata* (English yew),which is typical of Arts and Crafts gardens, *Thuja plicata* (western red cedar), or *Ilex aquifolium* (holly), provides a verdant backdrop throughout the year and adds a sense of permanence. Deciduous hedges introduce seasonal variety, but become see-through in the autumn unless they have been densely planted. Use prickly species such as the *Crataegus succulenta* var. *macrantha* (thorn) for added security, or *Fagus sylvatica* and *F. s.* Purpurea Group (common and purple beech), the dead leaves of which remain attached. For a thick perimeter hedge, plant a double-staggered row of trees spaced 36in apart, with 36in between the two rows. For a simple internal division, use a single row spaced 18in apart. To ensure quick results, use young trees, add plenty of organic manure when planting (spirng or fall are the best times), keep watered in dry spells, and apply a top dressing of fertilizer every spring. Apertures in hedges should preferably have an organic feel, such as a solid wooden frame and a gate.

Living plants can be used to divide your courtyard and produce interesting visual blocks. Hedges can be grown in curves, the thickness and height varied and

the top cut into shapes, for example, a wave pattern. An late 17th-century Dutch idea was to clip topiary designs on the top of a hedge. "Windows" offer a glimpse of further attractions, and a mixture of evergreen species creates an attractive foliage tapestry.

Formal living screens can also be made from a low-maintenance wall of bamboos, a row of espaliered fruit trees—perfect for an edible garden—or a pleached alley of *Carpinus* (hornbeam), as featured in the medieval courtyard, which will also encourage movement between the various compartments.

For an informal screen, you can either use a stand of small sapling trees or clumps of tall, non-invasive bamboos. Twining climbers such as *Ipomoea* (morning glory) are suitable for growing on uprights that are attached to a raised, horizontal piece of stainless steel tubing. The effect will be very futuristic.

Stepping stones (right), set in the grass that passes between an avenue of trees, entice you to move toward the gap in the hedge. This narrow entrance into another enclosed section of the garden creates a sense of mystery and evokes curiosity.

A formal hedge (left) provides a protective screen around a formal courtyard, the design of which is based on the repetition of squares and rectangles. Living boundaries such as this do much to soften the impact of hard geometric shapes and surfaces.

floors

The floor comprises the path network and some form of hard standing area on which the table and chairs are placed. The hard floor should be easily accessible from the house, although it need not be directly attached to it.

The floor shape should be in keeping with the garden style—a seating-area-cum-perimeter path in a classical courtyard, or a terrace in a Renaissance design—and the choice of material should reflect its use. Areas that receive a high level of traffic, such as patios, need to be constructed from stable, durable materials such as stone flags, paving slabs, tiles, bricks, paving slabs, pavoirs, poured concrete, or wood. Furthermore, the chosen material needs to be in keeping with the style of the courtyard—for example, brightly painted concrete has a Latin feel. Terracotta tiles or natural stone flags suit an arid garden, while wooden decking or white concrete are appropriate in a spa garden. Rubber matting gives a futuristic feel and granite slabs are low maintenance.

Raked gravel patterns (left) are a meaningful element in Japanese gardens, rather than a surface on which to walk. A similar effect is easy to achieve and makes a low-maintenance feature.

Black-and-white tiling (right) has a timeless elegance. Although the tiles can be arranged in any number of different patterns, using a predominance of white in a sheltered courtyard makes the area feel much lighter and airier. Tiles are also effective in uniting floor and walls, in this case by covering the steps leading from the French windows to the garden.

Simple, elegant, but effective (below, top) is a good motto for all aspects of garden design. The white stripes unite the horizontal flooring to the vertical white wall, while the yellow wall and collection of pots introduce contrasting color and a change in form.

The transition (below, bottom) from solid slate paving to gravel-covered bed is made easier on the eye and turned into a feature by introducing a double edging that contains a midpoint—the water-washed stones.

Paths provide access around the courtyard and should be routed to take in all the key elements in a way that uses space to the full. To add unity to the design, construct paths from the same material as the floor, but for contrast, use a loose material such as gravel or bark chips. Loose materials are inexpensive and are easy to lay—simply pour them over a permeable geotextile membrane that has been laid on the ground in order to prevent incorporation into the soil.

Solid surfaces cost more, both in materials and labor. They need to be set on a firm foundation of 4in, which usually involves soil excavation and importing a subsurface. This must be compacted and the levels corrected (to allow rainwater run-off) before the flooring material is bonded to it, either using mortar or drymix (a sand-and-cement mixture in the ratio of 4:1). This may sound complicated, but in fact it is relatively straightforward, and although it can be time consuming, something you can do yourself.

The sunburst mosaic (left) is made from thin, water-washed stones. Such mosaics are best laid by a professional, and may be used to create a special ambience within a part of the garden, which is reflected by additional ornaments. The seat here has a somewhat Arthurian look.

The stones (above) flow from the path into the pool. An artistic touch, which echoes the steps, is the arrangement of blue stones at the water's edge. The purple iris and the gray-blue hosta leaves pick up the cool colors.

The vivid colors (right) used for this crazy paving give the impression of a stained glass window laid horizontally. Using bright colors in a random pattern provides a lively setting for other features and ornaments, which should be simple and restrained in color and form.

Stone paving (above) is expensive, but adds a timeless elegance to any courtyard space. Reconstituted stone is a less expensive alternative that creates a very similar result.

A slightly surreal look (below) is created by the vivid green, moss-covered boulders, which have been placed near the path of cut log stepping stones set in wood chips.

The correct selection (right) and positioning of different flooring materials, together with appropriate planting, creates harmony and variety. The use of an urn as a water feature is a novel idea.

Creeping perennials (above) such as *Selaginella* can be effectively used to provide a transition between different types of flooring, the green of the leaves emphasizing the colors of the paving and brick. A country cottage style can be achieved by planting a range of species in gaps between paving.

Variety (below) and interest are evident in this floor, where a single material has been used. The designer has introduced tiles of different sizes and shapes and arranged them in various patterns. An alternative would be to introduce a limited number of different tiles to break up the expanse of a single color.

architectural
plants

Architectural plants are a part of the courtyard's overall framework and must provide a focus throughout the year. Therefore, while some species such as *Yucca gloriosa* have the additional attraction of striking flowers, the majority, such as *Corylus avellana* 'Contorta', have an eye-catching shape, or they have strong foliage form, for example *Phormium* 'Dazzler'. Others, such as *Dicksonia antarctica,* have both.

For the greatest impact when using architectural plants, buy large specimens. Admittedly, mature plants are more expensive, but if carefully positioned even a few will justify the cost by introducing points of interest and an instant sense of maturity.

Architectural plants are the stars of the garden and deserve to be arranged in a manner that emphasizes their stateliness. An

uncomplicated but very effective method is to display individual specimens in a bed or plant them in a container. Keep the surroundings low key, so that attention is focused on the plant and its impact is heightened. A plain, flat wall will provide a very effective backdrop. All architectural plants create an air of magic when lit at night, and in this case the wall provides the perfect screen for a dramatic shadow display.

Used near the interface of house and garden, structural plants are particularly effective in helping to link the architecture

Tree trunks (opposite) are similar in appearance to a row of columns, thereby helping to divide the garden into separate areas in a very subtle way. This distinction will be heightened by the fact that one area will be shaded by the tree canopy, and the others will not. At ground level, there is the opportunity to change the flooring to accommodate the soil. A further artistic touch would be to paint the tree trunks, or to select species with ornamental bark, such as *Betula utilis* var. *jacquemontii* 'Silver Shadow'.

Living sculptures (below) are made all the more impressive by the backdrop, a plain surface painted with colors that enhance those of the foliage, without detracting from the form of the plants. The solid, spiky, somewhat succulent agaves in the foreground have a collective mass that dominates the scene, contrasting with the lighter, more airy fronds of the palm in the background and the silver foliage and yellow flowers in front.

of the two areas. Large specimens may also be used as key plants in a larger planting display. Mature plants introduce another dimension of scale to a bed of smaller shrubs and herbaceous plants, which should be chosen for their foliage and flowers to harmonize and contrast with the architectural characteristics of the specimen. For example, ferns blend with *Musa basjoo* (banana), while *Phormium* and *Bergenia* contrast.

If you have a large enough bed—and budget—you can achieve very striking planting effects using only architectural specimens. To create a tropical courtyard or jungle-like lushness, use architectural plants with a wide range of foliage forms and heights, all planted relatively close together, for example *Trachycarpus fortuneii*, *Gunnera tictoria*, and *Myosotidium hortensia*. A bed of widely spaced specimens can generate a modern feel with unusual forms such as *Phyllostachys nigra*, *Acer palmatum* 'Dissectum' and *Cordyline* var. *australis* 'Torbay Dazzler', underplanted with a mixture of ornamental grasses.

Cacti (right) are perhaps the most architecturally diverse of all plants, and a cactus garden is a display of juxtaposed surreal forms. Yet it demonstrates that large plants with interesting and unusual shapes can be successfully associated with one another to create a garden full of organic sculpture. In a garden of architectural plants, the other features should act as complements, rather than as competing elements.

Topiary (below), devised by the ancient Romans, is a technique in which evergreen shrubs are clipped into geometric or animal shapes. In a small space it may be advisable to restrict the size of the topiary, and to give the shrubs added impact and height by planting them in a container that is appropriate to the style of the courtyard you are creating. Remember that the color of the container should match the green of the shrub's foliage.

water

Water is the most versatile of all design elements, and it can have a strong impact on the mood of the courtyard. The silent calm of a pool that reflects the scudding clouds heightens the natural tranquillity of an arid setting, the soft sound of gently falling water is soothing in romantic surroundings, and the powerful flume pouring into a canal brings dynamism to a modern courtyard.

Finding the correct site for a water feature is of considerable importance. The sound of moving water in the distance is intriguing, and will entice visitors further into the garden—as in the Mediterranean courtyard—while a fountain placed near a seating area in a hot climate, for example in an Islamic or Latin garden, will help to cool the air. However, as well as assessing the manner in which the water behaves and the moods it may engender, you will also need to consider the style of the water feature itself. There are many different types—indeed there is something to match every courtyard style. But the one you choose should be appropriate to your design—simplicity for Japanese, ornate for medieval, natural for tropical and so on.

The installation of fountains that stand alone or are wall-mounted is straightforward, particularly as many come in kit form. All you need to do is dig a hole for the water reservoir (sump), insert it in the ground and put in the pump. The next step is to fill it with water, cover, connect the pump hose to the fountain, and switch on. However, you should always have the electrical supply to the pump installed by a professional, and for ease of use, site the on/off switch inside the house, garage or shed.

The serenity (opposite) created by a flat, still expanse of water is counterbalanced by the surrounding exuberant display of drought-tolerant, architectural specimens. The ground cover of round boulders provides a transition. In hot and dry climates, water is precious, and a water feature has even more impact in terms of something unexpected but welcome.

Mirror-like (below), the water in this formal pool is used to reflect the exotic artwork at the far end. This is a most tranquil spot to sit and reflect, as the lily pads help to soften the display, while the stepping stones break up the long axis. Still pools are also very effective when they simply reflect the sky and moving clouds.

Pools are more complex, but they are also something you can make yourself. Informal or curved ponds are best lined with a sheet of rubber material placed on top of a padded underlay to prevent sharp stones from piercing it.

Formal pools with straight lines and angles, and those that have an intricate shape, are most easily constructed from shuttered concrete. As a precaution, put a rubber liner underneath, because if concrete does crack and leak, it is almost impossible to reseal. And remember, if you want to keep fish in a pool, it should be at least 3ft deep and have a fountain to aerate the water. (For the method of calculating the amount of flexible line and concrete needed for a pond, see below.)

Calculating Area for a Flexible Liner or Concrete

Liner To calculate the area of liner you need, multiply the length of your pool plus twice the maximum depth by the width of the pool plus twice the maximum depth. You will also need the same area of underlay.

Concrete To calculate the volume in cubic feet, simply multiply this area by the thickness of the concrete lining.

A sheet of water (left) falls from a hole in the brick wall in a most surprising fashion. The water's fluidity and sparkle brings a sense of calm to a corner of the garden that is planted with a display of plants in different shapes, colors and forms.

The Green Man (opposite, far left) cast in lead, adds a sense of place and style to a courtyard garden, without taking up valuable space. Wall-mounted fountains are very effective, because they provide a focus and the all-important sound of falling water, but because the flow is slow the noise is not overpowering.

A tiled seahorse (left) with twin water jets is a very attractive water feature, a piece of sculpture and a bit of fun all rolled into one.

Hieroglyphics (below left) make an interesting idea for ornamenting a wall. The rill into which the water drops links various sections of the garden, a technique that helps instill harmony and unity.

Vertical jets (bottom right) of water are very effective in bright sunlight— they catch the light and refract it, creating rainbows. They are also efficient at cooling the air.

lighting

Garden lighting is one of the most inconspicuous and most neglected structural elements of courtyard design, but it is vital if you want to use your courtyard once the sun has set.

Naked flames are both inexpensive and romantic. Hurricane lamps, hung in groups from a tree, look enchanting, while candles are best mounted in plain or stained glass holders to extend their burning time and prevent them being extinguished by a gust of wind. An attractive and simple alternative, suitable for a party, is to cut patterns in the sides of a square paper bag and set a tea candle into a handful of sand placed in the bottom of the bag. In winter, a brazier filled with burning logs brings warmth as well as gentle flickering light to tempt you outside on fine evenings.

The range of electric lights available is enormous, and if you are going to design

your own system, you will have to decide what it is you want to illuminate, and how. Use functional spread lights and border lights to illuminate access routes (as in the easy-care garden), borders and pool edges. For aesthetic effects, use different types of bulbs, each of which casts a different type of light. These might range from stark halogen to soft white. You could also use a range of different lighting techniques, either combining them or employing them individually. Uplights placed beneath specimen trees or architectural plants illuminate the structure and foliage, casting intriguing shadows in the wind, an effect that can be enhanced by using colored filters. Downlights should be used to illuminate sitting or entertaining areas; if they are directed through tree branches they will imitate moonlight. Use spotlights to pick out individual features such as statues, or set them in a pool to illuminate a

Uplights (left) may be an attractive feature in their own right, so be sure to select a style to match the surrounding materials. Of more importance, they are the perfect type of light to illuminate specific features or plants anywhere within the garden. They may also be used very effectively to define the edges of a path, or within pools and behind fountains.

As the lights are switched on (below left), the garden takes on a whole new persona. Uplights pick out the tree trunks, angled lights the rocks, and wall lights give overall illumination.

Downlights and uplights (below) are used together to transform a corner of this modern garden into a nighttime hideaway. The combination of lighting casts weird and wonderful shadows on the surface of the walls and creates exotic plant silhouettes. The canopies reflect and help to soften the light.

fountain. You can create silhouettes and shadows against walls by using ground-level lights positioned at an angle in front of the object. Surfaces that are decorative or interesting themselves can also be lit this way. Finally, strings of tiny lights look magical when wrapped around a tree trunk and scattered through the tree's branches,

while fiber-optic lights add a touch of the unusual. Whatever lighting system you choose, seek professional help with the installation of electric lights, unless you opt for the low-voltage systems suitable for amateur use, or solar powered lights, which you simply stick into the ground and can move around as needed.

decorative features
and effects

statues
and ornaments

Statues and ornaments influence the mood of the garden. They should not give the impression that they have been imposed, but rather that they are an integral part of the courtyard structure. Position is therefore of the utmost importance. A piece of sculpture should be attractive from all angles, at any time of the year, and blend in with, but stand out from, its surroundings. It is also necessary to consider views that will be seen from the house. And to make the most of a larger statue or ornament, it is worth considering lighting it at night.

Antique statues are expensive to purchase, but authentic-looking reproductions cast from reconstituted stone (cast concrete deteriorates) are an affordable substitute. To speed up weathering, you can smear the stone with yogurt or diluted manure. For an effective, additional touch, train strands of ivy over the stone.

Commissioning an artwork can also involve considerable outlay. An alternative is to create your own unique piece of art; for example, a row of driftwood branches hung with glass bottles will look stylish in a minimalist setting, and water-washed boulders cemented together in a cone shape, reminiscent of a cairn, make a positive statement in an arid environment.

For maximum impact, simple, bold pieces work best. Japanese gardens use ornament in moderation, but the result is always dramatic. Use this approach as your inspiration and position one large sculpture to create a specific effect—to make a "full

Ornaments can be amusing (above): This deer is constructed from wire and covered with moss and ivy. The garden is an example of how a range of different, but carefully selected, ornaments can provide a series of attractive effects.

A gentleman (left) casts his noble but sightless gaze over this courtyard. Stone busts and statues in human form bring a sense of timelessness to a garden, which, full of trees, shrubs, and flowers, is otherwise a dynamic, organic art form.

Sculpture inspired by mythology (right) is used to make a striking focal point in this classically influenced courtyard. The fountain's impact is doubled by the imaginative use of a mirror, which makes the space appear larger, and reveals the opposite side of the sculpture.

stop" at the end of a vista, provide counterpoint in an asymmetric layout, or a central feature within a formal space.

Topiary is living sculpture—box or yew that has been clipped into geometric shapes adds height and winter interest to a formal garden. The Japanese sculpt azaleas to look like natural rocks. In both cases, begin with small plants, and trim carefully until they are large enough to be clipped into a specific form.

For more variety, supplement the key ornament with a few small sculptures, such as cast bronzes or monoliths. Use bonsai if you want to have a mature tree in a tiny space. Remember, too, that artwork creates intriguing reflections in a still pool and lighting will bring art to life at night.

A beautiful, lichen-encrusted female (opposite left) brings a sense of grace and romance to this verdant corner of the garden. It is as important to consider a statue's backdrop as it is its position. The two elements should harmonize, with the background acting as a foil to display the piece.

A slate slab (top left) carved with calligraphy in an elegant script is a subtle but very effective ornament when positioned to peek out from the planting. The impact of this type of ornament set among foliage is often greatest when used in an understated manner.

The graceful curves (top right) and texture of the wooden bird appeal to the senses. The bird is of sufficient size to dominate its immediate surroundings, and so act as a focal point, uniting the planting and collection of smaller ornaments.

Wire spheres (right) are a simple yet effective visual addition to this gravel bed, dominating the planting and contrasting with the color of the gravel. As they are easily moved their position in the courtyard can be readily altered.

A decorative plaque (far right) on a wall enlivens a plain surface and draws attention to a particular corner of the garden. Surrounded by these plantings, it is evocative of romance.

special effects

Features for special effects should be objects that are out of the ordinary, even startling. A waterproofed television set in a hedge, an internal division constructed from a large fish tank, or a pair of curtains on a perimeter wall that open to reveal a fine view—all will generate good humored bewilderment and entertainment.

Fire has a relaxing, mesmeric quality, especially if it is associated with falling water. It is little used, but it is an inexpensive special effect that can be easily installed in a courtyard setting. You can use gas flares or make your own fire effects from lengths of flexible $^1\!/_3$ in copper pipe. First seal the pipe at one end and drill it with holes. Next, attach the pipe to a low-pressure propane gas bottle and regulator, using a rubber hose. Finally, lay the pipe in position horizontally, and conceal it under a several layers of gravel (earth will block the holes).

You can use this device to create a ring of fire around a large monolith, line paths with pillars of flame, or create a "will-of-the-wisp" in a flowerbed. Fire is also a novel form of garden lighting.

To maximize astonishment, hide special effects that will be triggered by unsuspecting guests. Joke fountains (which originated in the Italian Renaissance gardens) and mist units can be adapted to suit any garden style, although water jets are best restricted to courtyards in hot climates, where a soaking will be pleasantly cooling. Controlled by a solenoid (on/off switch), a timer, and a photoelectric cell, the jets will dampen unwary visitors from unusual angles when least expected. Place the cell so that the visitor breaks the beam when walking along a path, is about to sit on a bench, or is bending over to catch the fragrance of a flower. Once the beam is broken, the water remains on for a set period.

To create mists of surprises, follow the same principle, but exchange the water jet for a mist nozzle. Billowing mist looks dramatic in all weathers except fog, and instead of getting wet, the visitor hears a loud hissing noise before disappearing in a white cloud. Mist experiences may also be activated automatically. By setting the timer, you can make a statue belch forth "smoke" in the middle of a dinner party, make a tree disappear in a cloud of mist, or a pool spew out "steam."

Ice-blue ground glass (right), arranged in a spiral pattern that rises above the surface of the pool, gives the impression of bubbles coming up through the water. The carved head completes the surreal design.

By day (opposite), a corner of the garden is an attractive sculptural display of varied rocks and gravel, which, with the backdrop of bamboo and palm, has a slightly Japanese appeal.

As night falls (below), the garden space is transformed by a stunning special effect. From a gas container with regulator attached (the type used for barbecues), gas is supplied to a network of pipes hidden within the gravel. The gravel disperses the gas, so, when lit, it creates these spectacular sheets of flame, which have a raw, natural energy, evoking a powerful primeval feeling. The effect is most potent at night, but is also effective by day. (Note that the equipment for such displays should be installed by a professional.)

containers

Whether empty or brimming with plants, containers contribute to the style and mood of a courtyard and should be considered as part of the structure, rather than portable extras. Placement is the key to successful container planting.

A stone urn on a plinth can form the centerpiece in a formal garden, and a painted wicker basket adds rustic charm to a courtyard full of edible crops. A pair of pots introduces balance and a group creates dynamic asymmetry, while a single curved terracotta oil jar, set within a sea of gravel and surrounded by foliage plants, makes a low-maintenance focal point.

Planted containers create a transition between the hard landscaping and beds and borders, broadening the scope for planting in small spaces and enabling you to grow plants that require special soil. The range of materials and style of pots are endless, some needing more maintenance than others. For example, wooden Versailles tubs must be painted every year or so; terracotta, both glazed and unglazed, should be frost proof; and stone can be aged. You can also use recycled materials and objects: glazed square sinks as troughs for alpines; half barrels to hold camellias; old watering cans to house trailing annuals or wheelbarrows filled with lettuce plants.

When selecting the container for a planting display, consider the container and plants as complementary, but think of the plants as the stars. The container should have a simple, attractive shape and a color that will enhance the planting. The planting itself should be bold and decisive, with either a single specimen or several of the same species in each pot. To create a harmonious, larger display, choose a variety of pots and plants that complement and contrast with one another. (See the list of container-friendly plants on page 149.)

Contrasting textures and colors (right) have been introduced into this Mediterranean courtyard by simple, yet boldly shaped terracotta containers. Their curved form is accentuated by the use of a yucca and trailing pelargoniums.

All plants in containers will need regular watering and feeding. You can accomplish both jobs at once by using a liquid fertilizer, and save time by installing an automatic watering system. The container must hold sufficient soil to insulate plant roots from frost during the winter, and to sustain healthy growth. When the plant's roots have completely filled the container, the plant has become pot bound. To ensure further growth, it should be transplanted into a larger one.

Rectangles of slate (above) wired together make very attractive yet simply constructed containers. The arrangement of the four square planters adds mass to the display, while their regular form and dark gray color is a perfect foil for the domes of clipped box. This soft roundness is picked up by the surrounding water-washed stones, while their pale color provides another contrast with the slate.

Soft, bold harmony (left) is the key to this display. The rounded edges of the adobe walls meld with the curved form of the container, and the globe-like form of the cacti. This matches perfectly with the color scheme, which uses subtle earthy shades.

A contrast (left) between the very simple and the highly ornate. The lower container seems to be an organic extension of the house, while the other is not. However strange their juxtaposition, it works, aided by the continuity of planting. The idea of mixing different types of containers is one that is applicable to all garden styles, just as long as they suit the overall mood of the garden.

A stone trough (above), which looks as if it has been in situ since the house was built, has been converted from its original role as a water container into a planter. The transformation has all the more impact because it is planted with a mixture of brightly colored *Nicotiana*, which brings alive the natural beauty of the gray stone and the planter.

A stone urn (below) with the leering face of the ancient Greek god, Pan, and other classical devices, is an ornate plant container. Placed on top of a wall in a shady corner, the rich greens and architectural shapes of the fern foliage help to accentuate the detail of the face. Such urns may be carved from stone or cast from reconstituted stone. The latter are much less expensive.

Art and nature (right) combine as a rectangular stone trough is built around a large boulder. Mass planting of a single species adds to the contrast in this garden of surprises. In the distance there is a cast concrete container, which also demonstrates the ideal of mass planting.

Curved terracotta pots (bottom right) make them sculptural elements in their own right. Contrasting colors and their position in the embrace of a right-angle increase their impact.

shades
and awnings

The most substantial and expensive shelters offering protection from strong sunlight or rainfall are open-sided gazeboes and glazed summerhouses. (If heated and lit, they can be used all year.) Made from stone, brick or wood, they should be attractive to look at and provide views over the garden. Less costly and easy to construct are Japanese tea houses—bamboo screens nailed to a wooden post frame, or a large wooden or aluminum pergola. Pergolas can be free standing or propped against a wall with a roof of climbing plants. Alternatively, for lower maintenance, use wooden slats, dried palm leaves, or bamboo mats.

A metal arch (below) is roofed with natural, dried plant material. Such a roof may be made from various materials, including dried bamboo canes or palm leaves. The framework for the shade provides a support for climbing plants, and defines a window out over the garden.

A cloth awning (right) that projects out from the house is a perfect shading solution in a variable climate. It is easy to use when the weather is hot and sunny, and when not required it can be stored away. Using green material casts a restful light beneath the shade.

For natural, dappled shade, plant deciduous trees at a distance from the house in order to avoid the risk of root damage, or construct a bower from trellis work or woven willow wands. Train scented climbers through the branches to heighten the sensory experience.

Tents have many advantages. They are lightweight, easy to erect and maintain (wipe the material regularly and clean thoroughly once a year), and are perfect for entertaining and relaxing. They also suit many garden styles. An Arabian Nights retreat, with pitched canvas or marine acrylic roof, brings the romance of the desert to a courtyard, while brightly colored PVC or coated nylon supported on stainless steel poles is avant-garde. The color of the material will have an impact on the ambience of the garden— neutral, creamy white is most agreeable at a distance, with dominant colors best near the house. Colored fabrics also filter light, so choose a warm color such as yellow to reduce glare and to brighten up cloudy days.

Awnings are available as the traditional wall-mounted type that can be cranked up and down (often seen on café and store fronts) or irregularly shaped, sail-like structures set at an angle and supported on a wall and on poles. Sails are most effective when small, with several in a row. Yet simple is often best, and the umbrella on a wooden pole has a timeless elegance. It is easy to store when not in use and may be moved around the garden to bring a feeling of intimacy to dining and entertaining. Neutral-colored fabrics are best for toning down sunlight without being intrusive.

The dappled shade (left) cast by a roof of bamboo canes is in stark contrast to the white, sun-drenched walls of the courtyard. In a hot climate a form of shading is essential to enable you to use and enjoy your garden during the heat of the day.

A charming retreat (above) has been created using a traditional way of roofing with concave tiles and supporting beams. The hollow back wall will encourage a cooling breeze. There is even a curtain to draw if more privacy is required.

furniture

To enjoy your personal paradise to the full, functional garden furniture must be comfortable and assigned a semi-permanent position. For example, place a *chaise-longue* in the corner that catches evening light, and tables and chairs for outdoor dining near the door to the house.

The color of the furniture contributes to the mood of the courtyard garden. Natural wood, which suits all garden styles, ranges in color from sandy pine to rich tawny cedar, and acquires an attractive patina with age (it also takes on a silvery hue as it weathers). Painted furniture makes more of a visual impact. White is bold, while green is strident if set against a foliage backdrop, and should be avoided. Choose soft pastels to complement a flowering scheme.

The style and durability of furniture lies in the choice of materials. Hardwoods, such as iroko, teak, and cedar (from a sustainable source) require little maintenance—an oiling every few years is all that is usually necessary. Softwoods such as pine should be treated with stain or painted annually. Stainless steel and cast aluminum, appropriate for a modern look, need only an occasional polish. Elegant wrought-iron seats, perfect for a period setting, should be checked for rust and painted every year or so. Wicker and woven willow furniture must be protected from rain. Plastic furniture, although inexpensive and requiring no maintenance, does not weather well and is never stylish. However, it is useful to have a few lightweight chairs to take into the garden as necessary. Folding furniture such as bright, striped deck chairs,

Ornate cast ironwork (left) painted green and white helps to define the ambience and style of this courtyard. It combines with the evergreen foliage, gravel flooring, and clipped box to generate the timeless elegance of an Arts and Crafts garden from the end of the19th century. The white bench helps to lighten the courtyard and balance the variety of greens in the furniture and the foliage.

The rich color (top right) of the polished wood echoes the deep tones of the tiled floor, and contrasts with the decorative terracotta pot. The bench also brings a note of tranquillity to this corner of the courtyard.

Simply elegant (right), the bench has been constructed from three pieces of cut slate, providing a place to sit as well as a contrast to the soft planting.

A zany rocking chair (above), made from aluminum, is exactly the style of furniture needed to complement the bright colors and cheerful planting of this flamboyant garden.

The mass (left) of the stone table set of a solid base gives a sense of permanence. Slatted wooden benches balance the table, thus preventing the furniture from becoming too imposing. The table and benches have both weathered to a soft, mellow color that matches the walls.

Ornate benches (above) can be used to introduce a sense of formality into an otherwise informally planted part of the garden.

Table and chairs (opposite, left) find a natural home beneath this raised, classically inspired, climber-clad shelter. Elevating furniture in this way will provide a different view over the courtyard, as well as create a feature to be seen from other parts of the garden.

upright director's chairs, painted café table and chairs, or a hammock, are perfect choices where space is at a premium.

If furniture is permanently sited to play an ornamental role, materials, shapes, and styles will govern your choice: a turf or chamomile seat to provide a focal point, a circular wrought-iron seat around a tree trunk, or concrete bench lurking among foliage as a surprise. Seats built into retaining walls bring you closer to the planting. In some cases, comfort may be sacrificed for visual impact, but try to combine beauty with utility.

A sculpture (top right) or a seat? This modern piece, designed using clear lines and curves, has been positioned in the middle of a traditional garden to make a statement. It aptly demonstrates how, if carefully selected and positioned, furniture can fulfill a practical role as somewhere to sit, and an artistic role, as something to stimulate debate.

Perfect for a siesta (right), this bench with its Indian-looking rug and cushions is hidden away against a wall, just waiting for someone to take a nap away from the noonday heat. Furniture placement should take into account needs of privacy and escape.

plants
for courtyard gardens

Over 400 plants, used in the designs on pages 16–93, are described in the following pages. They have been selected because they are appropriate for small gardens, and courtyards in particular. The plants are arranged in categories to help you find plants for a specific purpose: for boundaries and divisions should you want a perimeter hedge or living internal screens; to clothe pergolas and trellises, fences and walls; and as eye-catching specimens. With the framework planting in place, you can then choose plants to provide seasonal color, foliage interest and ground cover.

Each plant description includes the Latin and common names where applicable, and the cultivation requirements to enable you to choose plants that suit your climate, aspect, and soil. For the less common species or cultivars, plants of similar type and color are suggested as alternatives at the end of the plant description.

Key

Light requirements

○ Full Sun

◗ Partial Shade

● Shade Loving

Moisture requirements

○ Well Drained

◗ Moist

● Wet

Special soil requirements (if applicable)

<7 needs acid soil

>7 needs alkaline soil

Seasonal display

Sp Spring

Su Summer

F Fall

Wi Winter

USDA Zones

Zone 1 Below -50°F

Zone 2 -50°F to -40°F

Zone 3 -40°F to -30°F

Zone 4 -30°F to -20°F

Zone 5 -20°F to -10°F

Zone 6 -10°F to 0°F

Zone 7 0°F to 10°F

Zone 8 10°F to 20°F

Zone 9 20°F to 30°F

Zone 10 30°F to 40°F

Zone 11 Above 40°F

Plant size

↕ Height

••• Spread

Plant categories

Enclosure and Division

Buxus sempervirens Box
○ △ 6-8 ⁝ 15ft ↔ 15ft
Evergreen, bushy shrub with a mass of small, oval, glossy, dark green leaves. Ideal for hedging, edging and topiary.

Carpinus betulus
Common hornbeam
○ △ 5-8 ⁝ 80ft ↔ 70ft
Deciduous tree. Gray, fluted trunk, yellow and orange leaves in the fall. Good on clay and chalk soils.

Crataegus succulenta var. macracantha Thorn
○ △ 4-8 ⁝ 16ft ↔ 16ft
Deciduous tree with long thorns. Clusters of white flowers in spring followed by bright crimson fruit. Colored leaves in the fall.

Fagus sylvatica Common beech
○ △ 5-7 ⁝ 80ft ↔ 65ft
Deciduous tree with pale green leaves, later dark green, then orangey-brown in the fall. Clipped hedges retain the dead leaves throughout the winter. *F. s.* Atropurpurea Group (purple beech) has blackish-purple leaves.

Ilex aquifolium English holly
○ △ 6-9 ⁝ 70ft ↔ 20ft
Evergreen erect tree with glossy, dark green leaves with sharp spines. If pollinated, female plants have bright red berries.

Phyllostachys bambusoides 'All Gold' Bamboo
○ △ 7-10 ⁝ 20-25ft ↔ indefinite
Evergreen, clump forming, with yellow canes sometimes striped green. Creates a perfect narrow division. Remove new sideshoots to prevent spreading.

Rosa glauca
○ △ 4-9 ⁝ 5-7ft ↔ 4-6ft
A medium-sized shrub with attractive reddish violet, almost thornless stems, purple-blue leaves. Clear pink flowers in mid summer, followed by red hips in the fall. Prune in spring.

Taxus baccata English yew
○ △ 5-9 ⁝ 30-70ft ↔ 25-30ft
Evergreen conifer with dark green, flattened needles. Female plants bear fleshy, bright red fruit in winter. Also makes a good free-standing specimen.

Thuja plicata Western red cedar
○ △ 5-9 ⁝ 70-100ft ↔ 15-25ft
Evergreen conifer. Ruddy brown bark peels with age. Dark green leaves have a pineapple aroma when crushed.

Specimen Trees and Shrubs

Arbutus unedo Strawberry tree
○ △ 7-9 ⁝ 25ft ↔ 25ft
Evergreen tree. Attractive bark, glossy, deep green leaves. In the fall, clusters of white, urn-shaped, pendant flowers appear with red, strawberry-like fruit.

Betula nigra Black birch
○ ◗ 4-8 ⁝ 60ft ↔ 30ft
Deciduous, fast-growing tree. Pinky-orange, shaggy bark is brown and rigid on mature trees. Leaves diamond-shaped, green, gray-green beneath.

Betula populifolia Gray birch
○ △ 4-8 ⁝ 20-40ft ↔ 15ft
Creamy white bark. Catkins in early spring, followed by dark green leaves that turn pale yellow in the fall.

Betula utilis var. jacquemontii Himalayan birch
○ △ 5-7 ⁝ 50ft ↔ 25-30ft
Deciduous, open-branched tree. One of the most beautiful birches. White stems and large, drooping, dark green leaves turn butter yellow in the fall.

Cercis siliquastrum Judas tree
○ △ 6-9 ⁝ 30ft ↔ 30ft
Clusters of bright pink, pea-like flowers in mid-spring before heart-shaped leaves, followed by long, purple-red, flat pods in summer.

Citrus aurantium Seville orange
○ △ <7 11 ⁝ 10-30ft ↔ 15-25ft
Widely branching evergreen with deep green leaves. Sweetly scented white flowers in spring followed by large, round, orange fruit. Alternative *C. nurantiifolia* 'Persian'

Citrus limon 'Meyer'
○ △ <7 11 ⁝ 10-30ft ↔ 15-25ft
Widely branching evergreen. Deep green, waxy, oval leaves, fragrant white flowers in spring followed by bitter yellow fruit.

Cordyline fruticosa Ti tree
○ △ Su 11 ⁝ 6-12ft ↔ 3-6ft
Evergreen, upright shrub. Long, lance-shaped, green leaves. Many forms, with leaf color ranging from purple-black through pink to yellow.

Cornus capitata
Bentham's cornel
○ △ <7 9-11 ⁝ 40ft ↔ 40ft
Semi-evergreen/evergreen spreading tree with oval, green-gray leaves. In spring, pale yellow bracts surround insignificant flowers, followed by large, strawberry-like red fruit. Alternative *C. kousa* Deciduous, leaves crimson-purple in the fall.

Cornus florida
Flowering dogwood
○ △ <7 5-9 ⁝ 20-30ft ↔ 20-30ft
Deciduous tree with showy white bracts in late spring, followed by red fruit in the fall. Oval, pointed, dark green leaves turn purple in the fall.

Cotinus coggygria 'Notcutt's Variety' Smoke bush
○ △ 4-8 ⁝ 10-15ft ↔ 10-15ft
Deciduous shrub with dark, purple-red foliage and smoky plumes of pink tinted flowers in spring.

Crinodendron hookerianum Lantern tree
◗ ◗ <7 9-11 ⁝ 10ft ↔ 23ft
Evergreen, stiff-branched shrub with red, lantern-shaped, pendulous flowers and dark green, narrow leaves. Requires a sheltered location with the plant base in cool shade.

Dacrydium cupressinum Red pine/Rimu
○ ◗ 9-10 ⁝ 30ft ↔ 4 ½ft
Slow growing but very graceful, conical shaped conifer. Should be planted in a prominent position. Alternative *D. franklinii*

Euonymus fortunei 'Emerald and Gold' Winter creeper
○ △ 4-9 ⁝ 6ft ↔ 10ft
Evergreen, bushy, mound forming shrub. Bright green leaves, tinged pink in winter, have golden yellow margins.

Ficus benghalensis Banyan
○ ◗ 10-11 ⁝ 100ft ↔ indefinite
Evergreen, spreading tree with tan colored trunk and reddish brown aerial roots. Dark green, leathery leaves. Beautiful red figs in pairs.

Garrya elliptica Silk tassel bush
○ △ 8-10 ⁝ 20ft ↔ 8-13ft
Evergreen, bushy shrub with wavy edged, leathery, dark green leaves. In winter the whole plant is draped with gray-green catkins, longer on the male than on the female.

Gymnocladus dioica Kentucky coffee tree
○ △ 4-9 ⁝ 70ft ↔ 50ft
Deciduous tree grown for its large leaves, pinkish when young, turning dark green in summer and yellow in the fall. Small, white, star-shaped flowers in early summer.

Ilex verticillata Winterberry
○ △ 3-9 ⁝ 6ft ↔ 4-5ft
Dense, suckering, deciduous shrub with oval, saw-toothed, bright green leaves. In the fall, female plants, if pollinated, bear a profusion of red berries that remain throughout the winter on the bare branches.

Juniperus communis 'Hibernica' Irish juniper
○ △ 3-8 ⁝ 10-15ft ↔ 12in
Vigorous columnar conifer. Mid to yellow-green, glossy, aromatic leaves. Round fleshy fruit, used to flavor gin, are green at first, then blue-gray, ripening to black in the third year.

Morus nigra Black mulberry
○ △ 5-8 ⁝ 40ft ↔ 50ft
Round-headed, deciduous tree. Deep green, heart-shaped leaves turn yellow in the fall. Succulent, edible, purple-red fruit ripens in late summer. Tree becomes gnarled with age.

Myrtus communis
Common myrtle
○ △ 8-9 ⁝ 10ft ↔ 8-10ft
Evergreen, dense, bushy shrub with oval, dark green, glossy aromatic leaves. Fragrant white flowers in mid-spring followed by dark purple berries. Can be trimmed much like box.

Olea europaea Olive
○ △ 9-11 ⁝ 30ft ↔ 30ft
Evergreen tree with oblong leaves, grey-green above, silvery beneath. Insignificant flowers, followed by edible green fruit that turns purple-black.

Pinus bungeana Lace-bark pine
○ ▶ 5-9 ⦂ 30ft · · 26ft
Bushy, slow growing conifer with dark green leaves and smooth, gray-green bark flaking to reveal creamy yellow patches darkening to red or purple.

Pinus mugo
Dwarf mountain pine
○ ◊ 2-9 ⦂ 10-15ft · · 15-25ft
Dense, bushy, spreading conifer with bright to dark green leaves and ornamental, medium-sized cones. The branches grow along the ground and then bend upward. 'Ophir' is a dwarf cultivar with a compact bun-shape. The winter foliage is golden yellow.

Platanus orientalis
Oriental plane
○ ◊ 7-9 ⦂ 80ft · · 80ft
Deciduous, spreading tree producing large, glossy, pale-green palmate leaves and multicolored, peeling bark. Inconspicuous flowers are followed by pendulous, spherical fruit clusters. Will tolerate polluted air.

Plumeria obtusa
○ ◊ 10-11 ⦂ 20ft · · 20ft
Evergreen, open tree with long, very dark green, glossy leaves and clusters of fragrant, pure white flowers with a faint yellow center.

Prunus x *subhirtella*
'Autumnalis' Higan cherry
○ ◊ 4-8 ⦂ 25ft · · 25ft
Deciduous spreading tree, bearing many small, white flowers tinged pink from late fall to early spring. The leaves are oval and dark green, turning yellow in the fall.

Pseudowintera axillaris
Heropito
○ ◊ 10-11 ⦂ 10-25ft · ·10-25ft
Evergreen, rounded shrub with oval leaves, lustrous mid green above, gray-blue beneath. From late spring on, clusters of tiny, greenish-yellow flowers, followed by equally tiny, bright red globular fruit. Alternative *Drimys lanceolata*

Quercus ilex
Holm oak/Holly oak
○ ◊ >7 7-9 ⦂ 80ft · · 80ft
Evergreen, dense, round-headed tree with dark, glossy green leaves, gray beneath. Small acorns in the fall. Can be wall trained.

Tabebuia aurea
Silver trumpet tree
○ ◊ 10-11 ⦂ 25-30ft · · 16ft
Slow growing evergreen with slender, irregular crown. Beautiful silvery gray-green, finger-like shaped leaves. Golden yellow flowers in clusters, all year. Alternative *T. impetiginosa*

Tamarix gallica Tamarisk
○ ◊ 9-11 ⦂ 12ft · · 20ft
Deciduous, spreading small tree with purple young shoots covered with tiny blue-gray leaves and sprays of pink flowers in summer.

Plants for Walls

Campsis radicans Trumpet vine
○ ◊ 5-9 ⦂ 40ft
Deciduous, woody-stemmed root climber with leaves composed of many leaflets. Trumpet-shaped, orange-scarlet or yellow flowers in late summer and early fall.

Chaenomeles japonica
Japanese quince
○ ◊ 5-9 ⦂ 3ft · · 6ft
Deciduous, thorny, spring-flowering shrub with bright red or red-orange flowers followed by yellow fruit. Can be untidy when free standing, but elegant when wall trained. *C. speciosa* is slightly larger and bears clusters of bright red flowers from late winter until the early spring.

Clematis armandii
○ ◊ 9 ⦂ 10-15ft · · 6-10ft
Evergreen, strong growing species with dark green, leathery leaves and fragrant white flowers in early spring. Requires a sheltered site on a sunny wall.

Clematis ligusticifolia
Woodbine
▶ ◊ 4-9 ⦂ 20ft · · 11ft
Deciduous, woody climber with slender stems, gray-green leaves, cup-shaped white flowers summer to fall.

Clematis montana
○ ◊ 6-9 ⦂ 22-40ft · · 6-10ft
Deciduous clematis with masses of single white flowers in late spring. Best planted where it can rampage. 'Elizabeth' has pale pink, vanilla scented flowers.

Clematis 'Nellie Moser'
▶ ◊ 9-11 ⦂ 11ft · · 3ft
Rose-mauve flowers with rich crimson stripe on each petal, in early summer. Best planted on a shady wall to prevent flowers bleaching.

Cydonia oblonga Quince
○ ◊ 4-9 ⦂ 15ft · · 15ft
Deciduous tree with oval, dark green leaves. In spring, the whole tree is covered with large, pale pink flowers followed by fragrant, deep yellow fruit, often used for making jelly.

Cytisus battandieri
Pineapple broom
○ ◊ 7-9 ⦂ 19ft · · 15ft
Semi-evergreen, open shrub with silver-green leaves divided into three leaflets. Grown for its racemes of pineapple-scented yellow flowers that appear from early to mid-summer.

Ficus carica Edible fig
○ ◊ >7 6-9 ⦂ 30ft · · 30ft
Deciduous, multi-stemmed shrub with large, deeply lobed, rough, light to dark green leaves. Edible fruit is produced in summer in hot climates.

Fremontodendron californicum
Flannel bush
○ ◊ 8-10 ⦂ 20ft · · 12ft
Vigorous, semi-evergreen shrub with masses of large, showy, bright yellow, saucer-shaped flowers in summer among dark green leaves. Best grown against a wall as it can be untidy.

Hydrangea anomala ssp. *petiolaris* Climbing hydrangea
▶ ◊ 5-8 ⦂ 30-50ft
Deciduous, woody stemmed, self-clinging climber with toothed, dark green leaves. In early summer, lacy clusters of tiny, cream-white flowers are produced on delicate stalks.

Jasminum officinale
Common Jasmine
○ ◊ 8-10 ⦂ 40ft
Semi-evergreen, woody-stemmed, twinning climber with dark green elaves composed of seven to nine leaflets. Grown for the deliciously scented clusters of small, white, star-shaped flowers that appear in summer and fall. *J. o.* 'Aureum' has bright green leaves irregularly splashed with yellow. Alternative *J. o.* f. *grandiflorum*

Lapageria rosea
Chilean bellflower
▶ ◊ 9-11 ⦂ 15ft
Evergreen, woody-stemmed, twinning climber with oval, leathery, dark green leaves. Groups of waxy, rose-crimson, pendant, bell-shaped flowers from spring to the fall.

Lathyrus sylvestris
Narrow-leaved everlasting pea
○ ◊ 6-9 ⦂ 6ft
Herbaceous perennial with leaves comprising a pair of leaflets terminating in a tendril. Racemes of rose-pink flowers are borne in summer and early fall. Provide support and cut down in late fall.

Magnolia grandiflora Bull bay
○ ◊ 7-9 ⦂ 30ft · · 30ft
Evergreen, rounded tree, often grown against a wall. Large, lemon-scented white flowers appear intermittently from spring to early fall.

Malus x *domestica* Apple
○ ◊ 6-9 ⦂ 30ft · · 30ft
Deciduous tree that can be wall trained into an espalier, cordon, or fan. Attractive, scented, white or pink flowers in spring are followed by large, sweet fruit that ripens in the fall.

Mangifera indica Mango
○ ◊ 10-11 ⦂ 80ft · · 100ft
Dome-shaped, evergreen tree with large, pointed, glossy, deep green leaves. Pyramidal clusters of tiny, pinkish-white flowers in winter, followed by edible fruit.

Mespilus germanica Medlar
○ ◊ 4-9 ⦂ 40ft · · 26ft
Deciduous, spreading tree with white flowers in spring and summer followed in the fall by brown fruit, which is eaten when half rotten.

Parthenocissus henryana
Silver vein creeper
▶ ◊ 7-8 ⦂ 30ft
Vigorous, deciduous, self-clinging climber. Leaves are green with white veins in summer, vivid red in the fall.

Parthenocissus tricuspidata
Boston ivy
▶ ◊ 4-8 ⦂ 40-60ft
Very vigorous, deciduous, self-clinging, woody-stemmed climber. Leaves lustrous green in summer, rich crimson to bright scarlet in the fall.

Passiflora vitifolia
Blue passion flower
○ △ 11 ⫶ 20-30ft
Vigorous climber with long, deep green leaves. Large, fragrant, vivid deep red flowers in summer, followed by small, velvety fruit.

Plumbago indica
Indian leadwort
○ △ 11 ⫶ 6ft ·· 3-6ft
Semi evergreen evergreen spreading shrub with mid green, oval leaves. Terminal racemes of red or pink primrose-shaped flowers in summer. Alternative *P. auriculata*

Prunus armeniaca Apricot
○ △ >7 3-8 ⫶ 25ft ·· 25ft
Deciduous, small, round-headed tree. White or pink tinged flowers in spring followed by orangey, edible fruit.

Prunus avium Gean/Bird cherry
○ △ >7 3-8 ⫶ 60-75ft ·· 30-40ft
Deciduous, spreading tree with red banded bark. Sprays of white flowers in spring followed by deep red fruit. Leaves bronze at first, dark green in summer, crimson in the fall.

Prunus cerasus Sour cherry
○ △ >7 3-8 ⫶ 15ft ·· 20ft
Deciduous, small, bushy tree. Dense clusters of white flowers in late spring followed by acid-tasting red or black fruit. A parent of the Morello cherry.

Prunus x domestica Plum
( ) ⌒ >7 5 8 ⫶ 16ft ·· 20ft
Deciduous, small, spineless tree with pinky-white flowers in spring followed by purple, edible fruit.

Prunus dulcis Almond
○ △ 7-8 ⫶ 25ft ·· 25ft
Deciduous, spreading tree bearing large rose-pink to white flowers in late winter and early spring.

Prunus persica Peach
○ △ >7 5-8 ⫶ 16ft ·· 20ft
Deciduous, small, bushy tree with medium-sized pale pink flowers in early spring followed by round, juicy fruit.

Punica granatum Pomegranate
○ △ 10-11 ⫶ 6-25ft ·· 6-25ft
Deciduous, rounded tree with narrow, oblong leaves. Bright red, funnel-shaped flowers appear in summer followed by spherical, edible fruit.

Pyrus communis Common pear
○ △ 4-8 ⫶ 30ft ·· 22ft
Deciduous, narrowly conical tree. White flowers appear with dark green leaves in mid- to late spring. Leaves turn orange-red in the fall.

Rosa 'Gloire de Dijon'
Old Glory Rose
○ △ 7-9 ⫶ 12ft ·· 8ft
Vigorous, stiffly branched, climbing tea or noisette rose. Large, fragrant, fully double, quartered rosette, cream-buff flowers from early summer to fall.

Rosa 'Maigold'
○ △ 7-9 ⫶ 8ft ·· 8ft
Vigorous, early flowering climbing rose with prickly arched stems. Large, fragrant, semi-double, cupped, bronze-yellow flowers.

Stauntonia hexaphylla
◗ △ 9-11 ⫶ 30ft
Evergreen, woody-stemmed, twinning climber with dark green leaves. Small, pale violet, fragrant, cup-shaped flowers in spring. Edible fruit.

Stephanotis floribunda
Wax flower
◗ △ 10-11 ⫶ 15ft
Evergreen climber with rope-like stems. Clusters of small, waxy, pure white, very fragrant flowers appear periodically throughout the year.

Thunbergia erecta
Bush clock vine
◗ △ 10 11 ⫶ 6 8ft
Sprawling climber or untidy shrub with funnel-shaped, violet-blue, yellow-throated flowers throughout the year. Alternative *T. grandiflora*

Trachelospermum asiaticum
○ △ 7-10 ⫶ 20ft
Evergreen, woody, many branched, twinning climber with masses of small, very fragrant, white, cartwheel-shaped flowers in summer.

Trachelospermum jasminoides
Confederate jasmine
○ △ 9 -10 ⫶ 28ft
Woody-stemmed, twinning, evergreen climber bearing clusters of very fragrant, small, white flowers on the ends of the shoots, in summer. Glossy, green, lance-shaped leaves.

Tropaeolum speciosum
Flame creeper
○ △ 8-10 ⫶ 15ft
Rhizomatous, wiry, creeping herbaceous, twinning climber with blue-green leaves. Bright scarlet flowers in summer followed by bright blue fruit surrounded by deep red calyces.

Architectural Specimens

Acer palmatum var. dissectum
Japanese maple
◗ △ 5-9 ⫶ 4ft ·· 5ft
Elegant, deciduous, low growing, mound forming tree. The deeply divided and feathery foliage is green in spring, then turns a brilliant orange-red or yellow. The best color is achieved on acid soil. *A. p.* var. *dissectum* 'Dissectum Atropurpureum Group', bronze-red or purple leaves turn scarlet in the fall. Alternative *A. p.* 'Dissectum Nigrum'

Agave americana 'Variegata'
Variegated century plant
○ △ 9-10 ⫶ 6ft ·· 6ft
Succulent perennial. Sword-shaped, blue-green leaves edged yellow rise vertically from a basal rosette. Tall flowering spike of white flowers in spring and summer. Alternative *A. parryi huachucensis*

Agave parviflora
○ △ 9 10 ⫶ 5ft ·· 20in
Succulent perennial with basal rosette and upright, dark green leaves with white marks and white fibers peeling from the margins. Spike of white, bell-shaped flowers in summer. Alternative *A. parryi couesii*

Agave utahensis
○ △ 9-11 ⫶ 9in ·· 6ft
Succulent perennial with basal rosette. Upright, spiny, blue-gray leaves tippped with long dark spine. Flower stem of yellow flowers in summer. Alternative *A. neomexicana*

Aloe vera Aloe
○ △ 9-11 ⫶ 2ft ·· indefinite
A clump forming perennial with thick, lance-like, mottled green leaves that are toothed along the margins. The flowering spikes, 3ft long, carry bell-shaped, deep yellow flowers in the winter and spring.

Chamaerops humilis
European fan palm
○ △ 10-11 ⫶ 5ft ·· 5ft
Low growing evergreen palm with elegant bright green to gray-green, fan-shaped leaves, and erect flowering spike of tiny yellow flowers in summer.

Chimonobambusa quadrangularis
Square-stemmed bamboo
○ △ 10-11 ⫶ 0-10ft ·· indefinite
Creeping bamboo with dark green, square canes, occasionally splashed purple, and lance-shaped leaves.

Cordyline australis
'Torbay Dazzler' Cabbage tree
○ △ 9-10 ⫶ 20-30ft ·· 6-9ft
Slow growing, evergreen tree usually with a single stem topped with a dense mass of sword-like leaves and large plumes of creamy white, fragrant flowers in early summer. Alternative *C. indivisa*

Cortaderia selloana
Pampas grass
○ △ 7-10 ⫶ 6-10ft ·· 4-5ft
Evergreen, clump forming perennial producing tussocks of gray-green, arching leaves. Cream or silver plumes on spikes 6-10ft long in late summer.

Corylus avellana 'Contorta'
Corkscrew hazel
○ △ 4-8 ⫶ 15-20ft ·· 15-20ft
Bushy deciduous shrub with twisted shoots and branches. Green, broad, sharply-toothed leaves have fall color. Yellow catkins in late winter.

Cyathea cooperi Tree fern
◗ △ 10-11 ⫶ to 40ft ·· to 20ft
A beautiful specimen for tropical gardens. The trunk is crowned with huge, light green, arching leaves divided into small, triangular-shaped leaflets.

Cynara cardunculus Cardoon
○ △ 7-9 ⫶ 8ft ·· 3-5ft
Stately perennial with large clumps of silver-gray, pointed, lobed leaves that arch gracefully. Massive stems carry purple-blue, thistle-like flowerheads.

Dicksonia antarctica
Man fern
◗ ◗ 9-10 ⫶ 30ft ·· 12ft
Evergreen tree fern with stout trunk covered in brown fibers and crowned with large, arching, glossy to green, finely divided fronds.

Dracaena marginata
Dragon tree
○ △ 10-11 ⦂ 15ft · · 3-6ft
Elegant, slow growing, erect tree with many branched, slender trunk. Narrow, strap-like leaves, green with red border.

Echinopsis spachiana
Torch cactus
○ △ 10-11 ⦂ 6ft · · 6ft
Clump forming perennial with thick, ribbed, glossy green stems and pale gold spines along the rib borders. White, fragrant, funnel-shaped flowers open on summer nights.

Echium vulgare Viper's bugloss
○ △ 3-8 ⦂ 2-3ft · · 3ft
Biennial with upright stems, narrow, lance-shaped, dark green leaves. From spring through summer, flowering spike is covered with small, deep blue or purplish, trumpet-shaped flowers.

Echium wildpretii
Tower of jewels
○ △ 9-11 ⦂ 8ft · · 3ft
Erect, unbranched biennial. Rosette of narrow, lance-shaped, silver leaves. In late spring and summer, compact spires bear small, red, funnel-shaped flowers.

Ensete ventricosum
Abyssinian banana
◡ △ 10-11 ⦂ 20ft · · 10ft
Evergreen perennial. Short, stout trunk crowned with palm-like leaves, reddish mid-rib. Flowers, intermittent, are reddish green with dark red bracts, followed by small, banana-like fruit.

Heliconia psittacorum
Parrot flower
◗ △ 10-11 ⦂ 6ft · · 3ft
Tufted perennial with long-stalked, deep green, banana-like leaves. In summer, exotic-looking orange flowers with green tips and narrow red-orange glossy bracts.

Livistona chinensis
Chinese fan palm
○ △ 10-11 ⦂ 40ft · · 23ft
Slow growing, evergreen palm. Stout trunk, elegant, glossy, fan-shaped, arching leaves. In summer, mature trees bear insignificant flowers followed by loose clusters of black, berry-like fruit.

Mahonia japonica
◗ ◗ 6-8 ⦂ 5-9ft · · 8-12ft
Upright, evergreen shrub with deep glossy green leaves of many spiny

leaflets that can turn red in direct sun. Long, spreading sprays of fragrant lemon-yellow flowers in winter, followed by blue-black berries. Alternative *M. bealei*

Musa basjoo Japanese banana
○ △ 7-11 ⦂ 10-15ft · · 6-8ft
Suckering, evergreen, palm-like perennial. Short trunk, broad, lance-like, bright green leaves up to 3ft long. Pale yellow flowers in summer followed by inedible green fruit.

Opuntia robusta Prickly pear
○ △ 10-11 ⦂ 15ft · · 15ft
Bushy cactus with silvery blue, flattened, segmented spiny stems. Yellow saucer-shaped flowers in spring and summer.
Alternative *O. compressa*

Pachycereus marginatus
Organ-pipe cactus
○ △ 10-11 ⦂ 22ft · · 10ft
Perennial, columnar cactus. Ribbed, shiny, branching stem with minute spines along the rib edges. White funnel-shaped flowers in summer.

Pandanus pygmaeus
Dwarf screw-pine
○ △ 10-11 ⦂ 3ft · · 2ft
Evergreen tree lacking a trunk. Narrow, beautifully marked leaves with horizontal yellow stripes.

Phormium 'Dazzler'
New Zealand flax
◗ △ 8-10 ⦂ 6-12ft · · 4-6ft
Evergreen, upright perennial with long, sword-shaped, stiff, dark green leaves vertically striped with red, bronze, salmon pink, and yellow. Panicles of tubular, dull red flowers in summer.
Alternative *P.* 'Dusky Chief'

Phyllostachys nigra
Black bamboo
○ △ 7-10 ⦂ 20-25ft · · indefinite
Clump forming bamboo with mid green leaves and arching canes, green at first, then mottled brown and black. *P. n.* var. *henonis* (Henon), canes bright green at first, later yellow-brown.

Pleioblastus variegatus
Dwarf white-striped bamboo
○ △ 7-11 ⦂ 4ft · · indefinite
Evergreen species with pale green canes carrying spiky tufts of narrow, slightly downy, striped leaves. Spreads fairly quickly and can be invasive.

Pritchardia pacifica Fan palm
○ △ 10-11 ⦂ 30ft · · 20ft
Slow growing, graceful fan palm with ribbed, brown-ringed trunk and crown of arching, multi-segmented leaves.

Protea cynaroides King protea
○ △ <7 9-10 ⦂ 5ft · · 5ft
Evergreen, rounded, bushy shrub with very large, spectacular, pink water lily-shaped flowerheads set in pink to red bracts, in spring and summer.

Selenicereus grandiflorus
Night-blooming cereus
◗ △ 10-11 ⦂ 12ft · · indefinite
Spreading cactus with long, slender ribbed stems bearing clusters of short spines and supportive aerial roots. Large white flowers open at night in summer.
Alternative *S. anthonyanus*

Trachycarpus fortunei
Windmill palm
○ △ 8-10 ⦂ 30-50ft · · 8-10ft
Evergreen palm with single trunk covered with fibers and crowned with large, arching, deeply divided, mid green fronds. Sprays of cream-yellow, fragrant flowers in early summer.

Yucca gloriosa Spanish dagger
○ △ 7-10 ⦂ 6-8ft · · 5-6ft
Evergreen shrub. Stout stem crowned with rosettes of blue-green to dark green leaves. Panicles of bell-shaped flowers on flowering spike in summer.
Alternative *Y. recurvifolia*

Yucca whipplei
Our Lord's candle
○ △ 7-9 ⦂ 5ft · · 3-4ft
Evergreen, almost stemless shrub. Forms a dense rosette of pointed, slender, blue-green leaves. In late spring, the 10ft flowering spike produces panicles of greenish-white, lemon-scented, bell-shaped flowers.

Overhead Cover.

Bougainvillea spp.
○ △ 11 ⦂ 25-40ft · · indefinite
A genus of spiny shrubs and vines with small oval leaves and small, tubular, short-lived flowers in clusters near the ends of the stems. The flowers are surrounded by brilliantly colored, long lasting bracts. 'Barbara Karst' is a vining cultivar with brilliant, vivid purplish-red bracts

Humulus lupulus Hops
○ △ 5-9 ⦂ 20ft
Herbaceous twinning climber with hairy stems and bristly, deeply lobed, light green, toothed leaves. Greenish female flowerheads in pendant clusters in late summer.

Ipomoea tricolor 'Heavenly Blue'
Common morning glory
○ △ 10-11 ⦂ 10-15ft
Short-lived, twinning perennial climber with soft, hairy stems, best grown as an annual. In summer, white throated, deep purple to blue-purple, funnel-shaped flowers.

Lonicera periclymenum
Common honeysuckle
○ △ 5-9 ⦂ 23ft
Deciduous, woody-stemmed twinning climber with oval leaves and fragrant, tubular, white and yellow flowers flushed pink and red, in spring and summer. 'Graham Thomas' has flowers that are white in bud, opening yellow.
Alternative *L. p.* 'Serotina'

Vitis coignetiae
Crimson glory vine
◗ △ 5-9 ⦂ 50ft
Vigorous, deciduous, woody-stemmed, tendril climber with large, heart-shaped leaves, dark green turning orange-purple brown and scarlet in the fall. Tiny, pale green flowers followed by inedible black berries.

Vitis vinifera Grape vine
○ △ 5-9 ⦂ 30ft
Leathery, dark green, lobed leaf, broadly rounded in outline, turns red in the fall. Tiny, pale green flowers in summer are followed by edible fruit.

Wisteria floribunda
Japanese wisteria
○ △ 5-9 ⦂ 30ft
Deciduous, twinning, woody-stemmed climber with light to mid green leaves of oval leaflets that appear with drooping racemes of fragrant, violet-blue, pea-like flowers in early summer. 'Alba' has white flowers.

Wisteria frutescens
American wisteria
○ △ 6-9 ⦂ 30ft
Deciduous, twinning, woody-stemmed climber with leaves of ovate leaflets. Racemes of fragrant flowers, pale lilac-purple with a yellow spot, in summer.

Wisteria sinensis
Chinese wisteria

○ △ 6-8 ┇ 100ft

Vigorous, deciduous, twinning, woody-stemmed climber. Leaves of 11 leaflets. Dense 8-12in racemes of fragrant, mauve-lilac or pale violet flowers are produced in early summer, followed by velvety pods. 'Alba' is a white flowered cultivar.

Foliage Plants

Acalypha wilkesiana
'Godseffiana' Copper leaf plant

○ ◗ 10-11 ┇ 15ft ·· 12ft

Woody shrub with large, concave, bronze-green leaves daubed red, purple and copper, almost as wide as long. Narrow, tail-like spikes of red flowers are borne intermittently. Alternative A. w. 'Louisiana Red'

Acanthus spinosus
Bear's breeches

○ △ 6-10 ┇ 4ft ·· 2ft

Herbaceous perennial with large, deeply cut, arching leaves with sharp spines. Spires of mauve-and-white, funnel-shaped flowers in summer. Protect crowns in the first winter after planting.

Adiantum pedatum
Northern maidenhair fern

◗ ◗ <7 3-8 ┇ 18in ·· 18in

Vigorous, semi-evergreen fern. Upright, slightly arching mid green, finger-like, divided fronds are slightly wavy. Remove fading fronds regularly.

Adiantum venustum
Maidenhair fern

◗ ◗ <7 4-8 ┇ 9in ·· 12in

Deciduous fern with pale green, delicate fronds tinged brown when young. Glossy stems bear many triangular leaflets that give a delicate, arching appearance. Best on acid soil. Alternative A. hispidulum

Aechmea fosteriana
Living vase

○ △ 10-11 ┇ 2ft ·· 12in

A bromeliad with a dramatically colored tubular vase of stiff, erect, light green leaves, banded purple-brown beneath. Flowering spike of red bracts and yellow flowers. Alternative A. fasciata

Alocasia sanderiana
Elephant ear

◗ △ 10-11 ┇ 3ft ·· 2ft

Evergreen, clump forming perennial grown for its striking, heart-shaped, wavy-edged, dark green leaves with white veins. Insignificant flower spike in summer.

Asplenium scolopendrium
Hart's-tongue fern

◗ ◗ 3-8 ┇ 12-24in ·· 10-20in

Evergreen semi-evergreen with tufts of light green, upright, lance-shaped leathery fronds. Suitable for limey soils.

Asplenium trichomanes
Maidenhair spleenwort

◗ ◗ 3-8 ┇ 6in ·· 6-12in

Semi-evergreen fern with long, slender, tapering fronds of dark green leaflets with rounded tips. Thin stems are dark glossy brown to black.

Athyrium filix-femina
Lady fern

◗ ◗ 4-9 ┇ 18-36in ·· 18-36in

Dainty, much divided, pale green, arching, lance-shaped fronds arising from erect rhizomes and divided into long, pointed leaflets.

Bergenia ciliata Elephant's ears

○ △ 5-8 ┇ 12-14in ·· 20in

Clump forming, semi-evergreen perennial with large, rounded, hairy leaves. In spring, clusters of white flowers that turn pink with age.

Blechnum chilense
Chilean hard fern

◗ ◗ 9-10 ┇ 12-36in ·· 12-24in

Evergreen semi-evergreen fern with a ring of lance-shaped, mid green, outer fronds heavily indented and arranged symmetrically, inside which is an inner ring of fringed, brown fronds.

Codiaeum variegatum
var. pictum Croton

○ △ 10-11 ┇ 4ft ·· 4ft

Evergreen, sparingly-branched, erect shrub with exotic, glossy, leathery leaves varying in shape and size. Coloring also varies, the variegation a mix of yellow, pink, orange and red.

Dryopteris filix-mas Male fern

● ◗ 4-8 ┇ 4ft ·· 3ft

Semi-evergreen deciduous fern with spear-shaped, finely divided, deep glossy green, arching fronds arranged in a shuttlecock shape.

Festuca glauca Gray fescue

○ △ 4-8 ┇ 6-12in ·· 8-10in

Tufty, evergreen perennial grass. Narrow leaves in shades from blue-green to silvery white, forming a domed mound. Stiff, upright stems with violet tinged flowering plumes in summer.

Gunnera tinctoria

○ ◗ 9-10 ┇ 5ft ·· 5ft

Perennial with large, rounded, puckered and lobed leaves. Tiny, reddish green flowers in early summer.

Hakonechloa macra 'Aureola'

○ △ 5-8 ┇ 16in ·· 18-24in

Slow growing perennial grass with purple stems and tapering, ribbon-like, arching leaves. Young leaves bright yellow, finely striped green, often aging to reddish brown.

Helictotrichon sempervirens
Blue oat grass

○ △ 4-9 ┇ 3-4ft ·· 2ft

Evergreen perennial with stiff, narrow, silver-blue leaves. Straw-colored flowering spikes appear in summer.

Hosta species and cultivars
Funkia

◗ △ 3-8

┇ & ·· See individual species

Genus of clump forming perennials grown primarily for their decorative foliage, useful as ground cover in shade, but slug damage is a problem. Flowering spikes are held well above the foliage in summer.

H. crispula ┇ 30in ·· 3ft
Large oval to heart-shaped, wavy edged leaves, dark green with irregular borders. Pale mauve, trumpet-shaped flowers. Alternative H. 'Crisoula'

H. fortunei var. **aureomarginata**
┇ 30-36in ·· 3ft
Oval to heart-shaped, mid green leaves with an irregular, creamy yellow edge. Violet, trumpet-shaped flowers. Will tolerate full sun.

H. 'Halcyon' ┇ 12in ·· 3ft
Heart-shaped, blue-gray leaves. Cluster of trumpet-shaped, violet-mauve flowers.

H. sieboldiana ┇ 3ft ·· 5ft
Large, blue-gray, heart-shaped leaves, puckered and deeply ribbed. Very pale lilac, trumpet-shaped flowers.

H. sieboldii ┇ 18in ·· 2ft
Vigorous. Mid to dark green, lance-shaped, round tipped leaves with white edges. Violet, trumpet-shaped flowers.

H. ventricosa ┇ 28in ·· 3ft
Glossy, dark green, heart-shaped leaves with slightly wavy edges. Deep purple, bell-shaped flowers.

Myosotidium hortensia
Chatham Island forget-me-not

◗ ◗ 8-9 ┇ 18-24in ·· 24in

Evergreen perennial. Large, glossy, ribbed, sometimes curled leaves. Large globes of blue forget-me-not flowers in summer. Fails to thrive when moved.

Neoregelia carolinae
Blushing bromeliad

◗ △ 10-11 ┇ 8-12in ·· 16-24in

Evergreen. Bright green, lustrous, strap-shaped, finely toothed, spiny leaves. In summer, clusters of compact, tubular blue-purple flowers with red bracts. Alternative N. 'Blue Bullis'

Onopordum acanthium
Cotton thistle/Scotch thistle

○ △ 6-9 ┇ 6ft ·· 3ft

Branching, slow growing, erect biennial. Large, lobed, spiny, bright silver-gray leaves. Deep purple flowerheads in summer.

Polystichum setiferum
Soft shield fern/Hedge fern

◗ ◗ 6-9 ┇ 2-4ft ·· 30-36in

Semi-evergreen evergreen with broadly lance-shaped, divided, soft textured, dark green fronds.

Smyrnium olusatrum
Alexanders

○ △ 9-10 ┇ 2-5ft ·· 3ft

Slow growing, upright biennial with shiny, bright green leaves. In late spring clusters of large, yellow-green flowers followed by smooth, black fruit.

Ground Cover

Ajuga reptans Bugle

○ ◗ 3-9 ┇ 6in ·· 3ft

Evergreen creeping perennial. Short spikes of bright blue flowers in spring. Spoon-shaped leaves are dark green. Will tolerate both sun and shade.

Alchemilla mollis Lady's mantle

◗ △ 4-7 ⡇ 20in · · 20in

Perennial. Rounded, pale green leaves, crinkled edges. Sprays of tiny green-yellow flowers in mid-summer.

Asarum canadense
Canadian wild ginger

◗ △ 2-8 ⡇ 4in · · 6in

Low growing perennial with leathery, dark green, oval leaves. Small brown-purple flowers with unpleasant smell, in spring.

Convolvulus sabatius
Moroccan convolvulus

○ △ 8-9 ⡇ 6-8in · · 12in

Trailing perennial with narrow stems covered with small, oval leaves. In summer and early fall, vibrant, blue-purple, trumpet-shaped flowers.

Dorotheanthus bellidiformis
Livingstone daisy

○ △ 11 ⡇ 6in · · 12in

Annual. Carpet of fleshy, lance-shaped, gray-green to green leaves. Dazzling small, daisy-like flowers in shades of red, orange, yellow, and pink.

Hedera helix English ivy

◗ △ 5-10 ⡇ 30ft · · 15ft

Self-clinging or trailing evergreen perennial. Dark green, glossy, lobed leaves with paler veins. Insignificant, pale green flowers in summer followed by black berries. May become invasive.

Hosta species

All species of *Hosta* can be used as effective ground cover. See Foliage Plants (page 147) for details.

Hypoestes phyllostachya
Polka-dot plant

○ △ 10-11 ⡇ 30in · · 30in

Evergreen perennial with deep green, heart-shaped leaves flecked with pink or purplish spots. Small, lavender, tubular-shaped flowers intermittently throughout the year.

Impatiens hawkeri
New Guinea impatiens

◗ △ 10-11 ⡇ 24in · · 24in

Herbaceous perennial usually grown as an annual. Reddish, succulent stems. Serrated, ovate leaves, red mid-rib. Large flowers are brilliant red. *I. platypetala* has shorter leaves and smaller, rich crimson flowers.

Lamium galeobdolon
Yellow archangel

○ △ 3-9 ⡇ 12in · · indefinite

Semi-evergreen perennial. Oval, mid green leaves marked silver. Small, yellow, hooded flowers in late spring. Can be invasive.

Mahonia aquifolium
Oregon grape

◗ △ 5-8 ⡇ 2-3ft · · 3-5ft

Evergreen shrub. Forms a dense thicket. Glossy green, oval leaflets often red or purple in winter. Yellow flowers in spring followed by blue-black berries.

Pereskia aculeata Leaf cactus

○ △ 10-11 ⡇ 30ft · · 15ft

Deciduous, spreading cactus with spiny stems. The thick, fleshy leaves are dark green with black spines. Large, fragrant, white, yellow, or pinkish flowers with orange centers appear throughout summer.

Phlox divaricata Blue phlox

◗ △ 4-8 ⡇ 12in · · 8in

Semi-evergreen, spreading perennial. Oval leaves. In early summer, clusters of lavender-blue, saucer-shaped flowers.

Pulmonaria officinalis
Jerusalem cowslip

◖ △ 4-8 ⡇ 10-12in · · 12-18in

Spreading, evergreen perennial. Bristly, heart-shaped, silver spotted leaves. Pink flowers, early to late spring, age to violet and blue. Shade tolerant. Alternative *P. o.* 'Sissinghurst White' has white flowers.

Rubus tricolor

○ △ 7-9 ⡇ 2ft · · 6ft

Evergreen shrub. Prostrate and arching shoots with soft red bristles. Dark green, glossy, oval, toothed leaves and white cup-shaped flowers in mid-summer. Edible black fruit.

Saxifraga cuneifolia
Lesser London pride

◗ ◗ 5-7 ⡇ 6-8in · · 12in

Evergreen perennial. Carpet of rounded-leaf rosettes, late spring to early summer. Panicles of tiny, white flowers with red, pink, or yellow spots.

Saxifraga sempervivum
Saxifrage

◗ △ 6-7 ⡇ 4-6in · · 4-6in

Hummock forming, evergreen perennial. Tufted silver-green leaves in tight rosettes. Racemes of deep red

flowers in early spring. Alternative *S. pensylvanica*

Tradescantia spathacea
Moses-in-a-Boat

○ △ 10-11 ⡇ 18in · · 18in

Clump forming perennial. Lance-shaped, stiff, succulent leaves on very short stems, deep green above, deep purple-red below. Small white flowers are inside two large, purple, boat-shaped bracts.

Tradescantia virginiana
Spiderwort

○ △ 5-9 ⡇ 13in · · 24in

Clump forming perennial with strap-shaped, green leaves tumbling over one another. From spring to early summer, clusters of triangular-shaped, blue, pink, or white flowers.

Tropaeolum majus Nasturtium

○ △ 10-11 ⡇ 12in · · 3ft

Fast growing, trailing annual. Bright green, round leaves. Trumpet-shaped flowers in all shades of red and yellow, from summer until the fall. Edible flowers and leaves.

Vinca minor Lesser periwinkle

◗ ◗ 4-9 ⡇ 12in · · 5ft

Prostrate, spreading, mat forming, evergreen sub-shrub. Stems covered with small, glossy, dark green, oval leaves. Small, purple-blue flowers, mid-spring to early summer.

Herbs

Achillea millefolium Yarrow

○ △ 3-9 ⡇ 32in · · 24in

Vigorous, upright perennial with fern-like foliage and small white flowers on large plate-like flowerheads in summer. Can be dried for winter decoration.

Allium sativum Garlic

○ △ 3-9 ⡇ 24in · · 8in

Grown as a culinary crop for its corms or cloves. Thin, lance-shaped, erect leaves. Often the flowerhead never opens beyond the bud stage, but tiny bulbs form between the flower buds.

Allium schoenoprasum Chives

○ △ 3-9 ⡇ 12in · · 2-4in

Hardy, clump forming bulb with narrow, aromatic, hollow, erect, dark green leaves. In summer, globes of tiny bell-shaped, edible purple flowers.

Anethum graveolens Dill

○ △ 8-9 ⡇ 2-5ft · · 12in

Upright annual with branching, fine, feathery, aromatic leaves. Flattened flowerheads of tiny, yellow-green flowers in summer.

Artemisia abrotanum
Lad's love/Southernwood

○ △ 5-8 ⡇ 2½ft · · 2½ft

Semi-evergreen deciduous bushy shrub with gray-green to silver-gray, aromatic leaves. Clusters of insignificant yellow flowers in late summer.

Artemisia absinthium
Wormwood

○ △ 4-8 ⡇ 3ft · · 4ft

Woody, evergreen, bushy perennial with finely divided, gray-green, aromatic leaves. In summer, tiny, insignificant gray flowerheads on long sprays. Inedible.

Chamaemelum nobile
Chamomile

○ △ 6-9 ⡇ 4in · · 18in

Evergreen, mat forming perennial. Short, aromatic, finely divided, bright green leaves. White daisy-like flowers with yellow centers in late summer.

Coriandrum sativum Coriander

○ △ 5-9 ⡇ 24in · · 12in

Tender, upright annual with white flowers in summer, grown for the aromatic, bright green leaves and seeds.

Foeniculum vulgare Fennel

○ △ 5-9 ⡇ 6ft · · 18in

Erect, branching perennial with finely divided, feathery, bright green leaves. Large, flat plates of small yellow flowers in summer. All parts of the plant are used for culinary purposes.

Hyssopus officinalis Hyssop

○ △ Su 6-9 ⡇ 24in · · 3ft

Semi-evergreen deciduous, upright, dense shrub. Bright green, narrow aromatic leaves. Dense clusters of dark blue flowers from mid-summer to early fall. Can be clipped for edging.

Laurus nobilis Sweet bay

○ △ 8-10 ⡇ 10-40ft · · 30ft

Untidy shrub that can be trimmed and shaped. Glossy, dark green, narrowly oval, very aromatic leaves. In spring, small, pale, star-shaped flowers followed by black fruit.

Lavandula angustifolia
Lavender
○ ◌ 5-8 ⇡ 12-36in ·· 12-48in
Evergreen, bushy shrub with narrow, aromatic, silver-gray leaves. Spikes of very fragrant, mauve-purple flowers in summer. *L. a.* 'Alba' has white flowers. Alternative *L.* 'Lady'

Lavandula stoechas
French lavender
○ ◌ 8-9 ⇡ 20-30in ·· 20-30in
Bushy, dense, evergreen shrub with narrow, silver-gray, aromatic leaves. In summer, flowering spikes of tiny, fragrant, deep purple flowers are capped with a feathery, showy bract.

Mentha spicata Spearmint
○ ◌ 3-8 ⇡ 18-24in ·· indefinite
Hardy perennial. Aromatic, dark green, serrated leaves, purple-mauve flowers in summer. Grow in a pot set in the ground to prevent spreading.

Mentha x piperita Peppermint
○ ◌ 3-9 ⇡ 18-24in ·· indefinite
Hardy perennial. Aromatic, oval, slightly toothed, mid green leaves. Reddish green stems bear spikes of small, purple flowers in summer.

Monarda citriodora
'Croftway Pink' Bee balm
◗ ◌ 4-8 ⇡ 3ft ·· 18in
Clump forming perennial with whorls of soft pink flowers in summer above aromatic, oval, toothed, mid green, hairy leaves.

Nepeta nervosa Catmint
○ ◌ 5-9 ⇡ 14in ·· 12in
Clump forming perennial. Arching aroma with pointed, lance shaped, mid green leaves. Small, pale-blue, tubular flowers from early to mid-summer.

Nepeta x faassenii Catmint
○ ◌ 4-8 ⇡ 18-24in ·· 8-24in
Bushy, clump forming perennial. Makes a good edging plant. Forms mounds of small, grayish-green leaves with loose spikes of soft, lavender-blue, tubular flowers in early summer.

Ocimum basilicum Basil
○ ◌ 9-10 ⇡ 18in ·· 4-10in
Tender, upright annual. Strongly aromatic, bright green, oval leaves that are widely used in Mediterranean cooking and salads. Do not allow to flower if using for cookng.

Origanum dictamnus
Dittany of Crete
○ ◌ 7-9 ⇡ 5-6in·· 16in
Spreading herbaceous perennial with a prostrate habit. Small, aromatic, white felted leaves and tiny flowers set within purplish bracts. Perfect for the rock garden; tea made from the leaves is considered a panacea.

Origanum majorana
Sweet marjoram
○ ◌ 7-9 ⇡ 12-36in·· 12-18in
Sub-shrub often grown as an annual. Highly aromatic, round, pale-green leaves. Tiny white flowers in summer.

Origanum vulgare
Wild marjoram
○ ◌ 5-9 ⇡ 18in ·· 18in
Spreading, mat forming perennial. Dark green, aromatic leaves, slightly hairy. In a sunny position the leaves gain a very pungent flavor. Clusters of tiny, tubular, mauve flowers in summer. *O. v.* ssp. *hirtum* (Greek oregano), hairy, gray-green leaves, tubular white flowers in summer

Osmorhiza longistylis
Sweet cicely
○ ◌ Su 4-8 ⇡ 18-36in ·· 18-36in
Deciduous perennial. Inconspicuous white flowers in loose, flat, plate-like heads. Oval leaves in groups of three. The whole plant smells of anise.

Petroselinum crispum Parsley
○ ◌ 5-8 ⇡ 12-18in ·· 12in
Hardy biennial. Bright green, curly, mildly flavored leaves. Flat plates of small, cream-white flowers in summer.

Phlomis fruticosa
Jerusalem sage
○ ◌ 8-9 ⇡ 4ft ·· 4ft
Spreading, evergreen shrub with upright shoots. Lance-shaped, sage-like, gray-green, silver-edged leaves. Deep yellow-gold flowers in summer.

Rosmarinus officinalis
Rosemary
○ ◌ 8-10 ⇡ 5-6ft ·· 5ft
Dense, bushy, evergreen shrub. Aromatic, narrow, gray-green, needle-like leaves, silver beneath. Small, purplish-blue flowers from mid-spring to early summer.

Ruta graveolens Rue
○ ◌ 5-9 ⇡ 24-36in ·· 24-30in
Bushy, compact, evergreen sub-shrub. Pungent, finely-divided, blue-green leaves, greenish-yellow flowers in summer. Can cause irritating skin rash when skin is exposed to sunlight.

Santolina chamaecyparissus
Cotton lavender
○ ◌ 6-9 ⇡ 30in ·· 3ft
Evergreen, dense, rounded shrub. Narrowly oblong, white leaves on gray-white, felted stems. From mid to late summer, bright yellow button flowers.

Stachys officinalis Betony
○ ◌ 5-8 ⇡ 18-24in ·· 12-18in
Mat forming perennial with oval, mid green, round-toothed leaves. In summer, clusters of pink, purple, or white tubular flowers appear on sturdy stems. Inedible.

Symphytum officinale Comfrey
○ ◌ 3-9 ⇡ 3ft ·· 3ft
Vigorous, coarse, upright perennial with lance-shaped, hairy, rich green leaves. Creamy yellow or purplish flowers on hairy stems, in summer. Can be made into a liquid manure.

Tanacetum cinerariifolium
Pyrethrum
○ ◌ 4-9 ⇡ 12-15in ·· 8in
Hardy perennial. Finely divided, gray-green leaves, white beneath. Long flowering stalks crowned with daisy-like flowers, white with a yellow center, in summer. Alternative *T. argenteum*

Tanacetum parthenium
Featherfew
○ ◌ 4-9 ⇡ 8-18in ·· 8-18in
Moderately fast growing, short-lived, bushy perennial often grown as an annual. Aromatic, lobed, mid green leaves. Small, daisy-like, yellow-centered white flowerheads in summer.

Tanacetum vulgare Tansy
○ ◌ 4-9 ⇡ 3ft ·· 12-24in
Hardy perennial. Aromatic, deeply indented, dark green, toothed leaves. Yellow button-like flowers in late summer. Inedible.

Thymus vulgaris Garden thyme
○ ◌ 4-9 ⇡ 6-12in ·· 16in
This is the thyme everyone knows. A bushy, mat forming, hardy, evergreen perennial with thin, deep green,

aromatic leaves. Masses of mauve flowers in summer.

Verbena officinalis Vervain
○ ◌ 4-9 ⇡ 2-3ft ·· 12in
Upright, hardy perennial. Bright green, hairy, deeply divided leaves. Small, pale lilac flowers in summer. Avoid using during pregnancy.

Container Plants

Agapanthus 'Albatross'
African Lily
○ ◗ Su 9-10 ⇡ 3ft ·· 20in
Clump forming, evergreen perennial. Large, dense globes of white flowers on strong stems in late summer. Strap-shaped, broad, dark green leaves. Headbourne Hybrids have white, deep or pale blue flowers in summer and are very hardy (6-9).

Amaryllis belladonna
Belladonna lily
○ ◌ 8-10 ⇡ 20-32in ·· 12-18in
Fall flowering bulb. Large, bright pink, trumpet-shaped flowers on a purple stem. Strap-shaped leaves appear after the flowers.

Bracteantha bracteata
Golden everlasting/Strawflower
○ ◌ 10-11 ⇡ 1-4ft ·· 8-12in
Perennial commonly grown as an annual. Papery, daisy-like flowerheads, yellow, orange, red to pink and white, in summer. Ideal for dried flowers.

Camellia saluenensis Camellia
◗ ◌ 7-9 ⇡ 12ft ·· 12ft
Fast growing, evergreen shrub with lance-shaped, dark green leaves. White to rose-red flowers in early spring. Alternative *C. sinensis*

Canna indica Canna lily
○ ◗ 8-10 ⇡ 6ft ·· 18-24in
Showy, rhizomatous perennial. Large, deep green, veined, paddle-like leaves. In summer, bold spike of large, orchid-like, bright red flowers. Alternative *C.* 'Red King Humbert'

Cistus ladanifer Rock rose
○ ◌ 8-10 ⇡ 5-6ft ·· 4-5ft
Leggy, upright, evergreen shrub. Dark green, narrow, aromatic, sticky leaves. Large, white, cup-shaped flowers with central red markings, in early summer.

Crocus biflorus
○ △ 4-8 ⁝ 14in · · 1-3in
Early spring corm. Upright, white-purple flowers, yellow throats, purple striped outside. Narrow leaves with a white stripe.

Cyclamen hederifolium
⬗ △ 8-9 ⁝ 4in · · 6-10in
Fall flowering tuber. Pale to deep pink flowers, heart-shaped, ivy-like leaves patterned in silvery green.

Dianthus caryophyllus
Carnation
○ △ 5-9 ⁝ 30in · · 18in
Loosely tufted, upright perennial with narrow, silver-gray leaves. Clusters of very fragrant, bright pink-purple flowers in summer. Hardiness varies with selection. Alternative
D. c. 'Grenadin Hybrids'

Epimedium perralderianum
Bishop's miter
⬗ △ 5-8 ⁝ 10-14in · · 20-24in
Evergreen perennial. Large leaves of 3-toothed leaflets, bronze when young, later glossy green. In spring, clusters of small, pendent, bright yellow flowers.

Eryngium bourgatii Sea holly
○ △ 5-9 ⁝ 12-24in · · 12-18in
Clump forming perennial. Curved, prickly, jagged leaves, veined and silver-spangled. Blue stems crowned with thistle-like, blue-green, then lilac-blue flowers from mid- to late summer.

Erythronium americanum
Yellow adder's tongue
⬗ △ Sp 3-9 ⁝ 2-10in · · 2-3in
Spring flowering bulb with pendant yellow flowers, bronze tinted on outside, bright yellow inside, on brown stalks above a pair of semi-erect, mottled green-and-brown basal leaves.

Erythronium californicum
Californian fawn lily
⬗ △ Sp 3-9 ⁝ 6-18in · · 4-6in
Spring flowering bulb. Dark green, glossy leaves. Flowering stalks bear white or cream-white flowers with orange-brown marks, recurved petals. Alternative *E. c.* 'White Beauty'

Erythronium dens-canis
Dog's-tooth violet
⬗ △ Sp 3-9 ⁝ 4-6in · · 4in
Spring flowering bulb. Mottled green leaves, nodding, pink-purple or white flowers with recurved petals.

Fritillaria imperialis
Crown imperial
○ △ 5-9 ⁝ 2-4ft · · 8-12in
Spring flowering bulb. Clusters of twisted, glossy leaves. Ring of pendulous, bell-shaped, orange flowers is capped by tuft of leaves.

Hamamelis virginiana
Virginian witch hazel
○ △ <7 4-8 ⁝ 13ft · · 13ft
Deciduous, upright, open, small tree. Small, fragrant, spidery yellow flowers appear on the bare branches in winter. Broadly oval leaves turn yellow in fall.

Hedychium gardnerianum
Kahili ginger
○ ◗ 9-10 ⁝ 5-6ft · · 30in
Upright, rhizomatous perennial with lance-shaped, gray-green leaves. From late summer to early fall, the flowering spike bears many delicate, butterfly-like, fragrant, lemon-yellow and red flowers.

Hemerocallis citrina Day lily
○ ◗ 3-9 ⁝ 30in · · 30in
Vigorous, clump forming perennial. Dark green, strap-shaped leaves, fragrant, lemon-yellow, trumpet-shaped flowers in succession in mid-summer.

Hibiscus schizopetalus
Japanese hibiscus
○ △ 10-11 ⁝ 10ft · · 6ft
Large, evergreen shrub with graceful drooping branches, small heart-shaped, deep green leaves. Pendent scarlet to pink flowers in summer.

Hosta undulata var. albomarginata Plantain lily
⬗ △ 3-8 ⁝ 20-24in · · 20-24in
Graceful perennial with dark green, heart-shaped leaves with an irregular white border. Bell-shaped, mauve flowers on a tall stalk in early summer.

Iris germanica
○ △ 4-9 ⁝ 2-4ft · · indefinite
Rhizomatous bearded iris. Arching, sword-like leaves. Stems of up to six yellow flowers, bearded blue-purple to violet, late spring to early summer.

Isoplexis canariensis
○ △ 10-11 ⁝ 5ft · · 30in
Evergreen, rounded shrub. In summer, beautiful foxglove-like red to orange-brown flowers on dense, upright, spikes. Leaves strap-like.

Kniphofia caulescens
Red-hot poker
○ △ 6-9 ⁝ 4ft · · 24in
Evergreen, upright perennial. Coarse-edged, arching, narrow, lance-shaped, blue-green leaves. Stout stems with terminal flower spikes of small, tubular reddish-pink flowers in the fall.

Lilium martagon Turk's-cap lily
○ △ 3-8 ⁝ 3-5ft · · 6-10in
Summer flowering bulb. Lance-shaped, oval leaves, scented, turkscap flowers in pink or purple with darker spots.

Linaria purpurea Toadflax
○ △ 5-8 ⁝ 30-36in · · 12-18in
Upright perennial with narrow, oval, gray-green leaves. In mid to late summer racemes of tiny, snapdragon-like, purple-blue flowers, with touches of white at the throat.

Magnolia stellata Star magnolia
○ △ 5-9 ⁝ 8-10ft · · 3-4in
Deciduous, bushy shrub with gray-green flower buds opening in early spring to white, star-shaped flowers. Narrow, deep green leaves follow.

Narcissus poeticus
Pheasant's eye narcissus
○ △ 4-9 ⁝ 9-17in · · 3-4in
Late spring flowering bulb with fragrant flowers comprising small, shallow, yellow to orange cup with a red rim and glistening white collar. Narrow, erect, gray-green leaves. Alternative *N. p.* 'Actaea'

Neoregelia ampullaceae
Bromeliad
⬗ ◗ 10-11 ⁝ 6in · · 6in
Beautiful small, elegant bromeliad with light green, strap-like leaves spotted reddish brown. Lovely violet flowers complement the green leaves.

Nerium oleander 'Hawaii'
Oleander
○ △ 9-11 ⁝ 6ft · · 6ft
Drought tolerant, upright, dwarf bush evergreen shrub with leathery, dark green leaves. Flaring funnel-shaped, deep salmon-pink flowers from spring to the fall. Alternative
N. o. 'Little Red'

Nicotiana alata
Tobacco plant
○ △ 10-11 ⁝ 30in · · 12in
A rosette forming perennial commonly grown as an annual. Clusters of tubular, cream-white flowers borne in late summer that are very fragrant in the evening. The leaves are oval and mid green.

Ophiopogon planiscapus 'Nigrescens' Black mondo grass
○ △ 6-10 ⁝ 6-12in · · 12in
Evergreen, clump forming, spreading perennial. Grown mainly for narrow, upright, almost black, grass-like leaves. Racemes of small, mauve flowers in summer are followed by small, shiny black berries.

Pelargonium 'Voodoo'
Geranium
○ △ 10-11 ⁝ 24in · · 10in
Evergreen, upright, fleshy perennial, more correctly known as a zonal pelargonium. Large, wine-red flowers with dark purple centers are produced throughout the summer. Round, lobed, dark green leaves.

Phormium tenax Purpureum Group New Zealand flax
⬗ △ 9-10 ⁝ 6-12ft · · 4-6ft
Evergreen, upright perennial with tufts of long, sword-shaped, stiff reddish-purple to dark copper leaves. Short, purple-blue flowering spike produces panicles of tubular, reddish flowers in summer.

Rhododendron yakushimanum
⬗ △ 5-9 ⁝ 3ft · · 5ft
Neat, compact, dome-shaped evergreen. Oval leaves, brown felted beneath, are silvery at first and mature to very deep green. Funnel-shaped pink flowers, green-flecked within, fade to white in late spring. *R.y.* 'Bambi' has red buds opening to pale pink flowers flushed with yellow. *R.y.* 'Koichiro Wada' has rose pink flower buds opening to clear white flowers.

Romneya coulteri
Californian tree poppy
○ △ 7-8 ⁝ 4-8ft · · 4-8ft
Bushy, vigorous summer flowering sub-shrub grown for its large, fragrant, papery white flowers with prominent yellow centers. The leaves are gray and deeply divided.

Rosa 'Coral Dawn'
○ △ 4-9 ⁝ 12ft · · 6ft
Modern climbing rose with dark green leaflets. Clumps of coral-pink, semi-double flowers in summer; repeats in the fall. Will tolerate a shady wall.

Rosa gallica 'Versicolor'
Rosa Mundi

○ ◇ 3-9 ⁝ 30in · · 3ft

Old, well-loved rose, neat and bushy.
Semi-double, slightly scented, flat
flowers, rose-red striped with white.

Rosa 'Indigo'

○ ◇ 4-9 ⁝ 4ft · · 2ft

Old fashioned rose of upright habit.
Richly scented, vicious purple, goblet-
shaped flowers on long stems. Dark
green foliage, tinged dark red.

Sansevieria trifasciata
Snake plant

○ ◇ 10-11 ⁝ 3-4ft · · 4in

Tender perennial. Rosette of erect,
fleshy, pointed, stiff leaves, light silver-
green with jagged, deep green vertical
bands.

Strelitzia reginae
Bird of paradise

○ ◇ 10-11 ⁝ 3-6ft · · 30in

Evergreen, clump forming perennial.
Long, gray-green, paddle-like leaves.
Exotic, beak-like, orange and blue
flowers surrounded by red-edged, boat-
shaped bracts, mainly in spring.

Taxus baccata 'Fastigiata'
Irish yew

○ ◇ 7-8 ⁝ 30-50ft · · 12-15ft

Evergreen conifer. Erect branches, dark
green, flattened, needle-like leaves.
Cup-shaped, fleshy red fruit in winter.

Bulbs

Allium cristophii

○ ◇ Su 5-8 ⁝ 16-20in · · 6in

Striking summer-flowering bulb. Tall
flower stem, on top of which is a large
globe of star-shaped, purple flowers.
Gray, hairy leaves, semi-erect.

Allium ursinum
Wild garlic

◗ ◇ Sp 4-8 ⁝ 12-18in · · 12-18in

Hardy bulb with broad, strap-like,
bright green leaves that smell strongly
of garlic if crushed. The flower spike is
crowned with a cluster of small, starry-
white flowers.

Anemone coronaria Windflower

○ ◇ Sp 6-9 ⁝ 6-18in · · 6in

Parsley-like, semi-erect, divided leaves.
Large, shallow, cup-shaped flowers.
Color varies from white through blue to

purple and red. The hardiness varies
with the selection.

Bulbocodium vernu

○ ◇ Sp 3-9 ⁝ 1¼-1½in · · 1¼-2in

Spring-flowering corm. Reddish-
purple, widely funnel-shaped, stemless
flowers. Narrow leaves appear later,
and die down in summer

Cardiocrinum giganteum
Giant lily

◗ ◗ Su 7-9 ⁝ 10ft · · 30-42in

Stout, leafy stem topped with flowering
spike of pendent, long, cream-white
trumpets streaked purple-red inside.

Chinodoxa forbesii 'Pink Giant'
Glory-of-the-snow

○ ◇ Sp 3-9 ⁝ 6-8in · · 1½in

Early spring-flowering bulb with two
semi-erect, narrow leaves. Flowering
stem produces spike of star-shaped,
white-eyed, flat pink flowers.

Colchicum autumnale
Meadow saffron

○ ◇ F 4-9 ⁝ 4-6in · · 4-6in

Wine-glass-shaped, mauve flowers
followed by large, strap-shaped leaves.
'Waterlily' has double flowers.

Crocosmia x crocosmiiflora
'George Davison'
Montbretia

○ ◇ Su 6-9 ⁝ 24in · · 8in

Vigorous, clump forming, mid to late
summer flowering bulb. Sprays of
yellow-orange, funnel-shaped flowers
among dense clumps of narrow, sword-
shaped leaves. Can be invasive.

Crocus sativus Saffron crocus

○ ◇ F 5-8 ⁝ 6in · · 6in

Narrow basal leaves appear at the same
time as the purple, saucer-shaped
flowers. Flowers have dark purple
veining and bright red stigmas, which
yield saffron.

Crocus tommasinianus

○ ◇ Wi/Sp 3-8 ⁝ 3-4in · · 2in

Late winter to early spring flowering
corm. Slender, funnel-shaped flowers.
Petals pale lilac to dark purple, orange
center. Leaves have white central vein.

Crocus vernus Dutch crocus

○ ◇ Sp 3-8 ⁝ 4in · · 2in

Goblet-shaped flowers, striped or in
shades of white, purple or violet.
Central stigma is orange or yellow.

Cyclamen coum

◗ ◇ Wi/Sp 5-9 ⁝ 4in · · 2-4in

Winter/spring-flowering tuber. Bright,
rich crimson flowers, darkly stained at
the mouth. Rounded, deep green or
silver patterned leaves appear either
before or at the same time as the
flowers appear.

Dactylorhiza majalis
Western marsh orchid

○ ◇ Sp 6-8 ⁝ 30in · · 8in

Deciduous, terrestrial orchid. Long,
lance-shaped, green leaves, sometimes
spotted pink. Pyramidal dense cluster
of lilac to magenta tubular flowers with
recurved lip.

Fritillaria meleagris
Snake's-head fritillary

○ ◗ Sp 3-8 ⁝ 12in · · 2-3in

Slender, narrow, gray-green leaves.
Solitary, bell-shaped, white or
checkered purple pendent flowers on
slender stems.

Fritillaria pallidiflora Fritillary

○ ◇ Sp 5-8 ⁝ 12-18in · · 4-6in

Lance-shaped, gray-green leaves in
pairs. Bell-shaped, creamy yellow to
greenish yellow flowers patterned
brownish red within.

Galanthus nivalis
Common snowdrop

○ ◇ W/Sp 3-8 ⁝ 4-6in · · 2-3in

Pendent white flowers on a slender
stem in late winter. Large outer petals
and smaller inner ones form an upside-
down cup marked green. Narrow, semi-
erect, strap-shaped, gray-green leaves.

Hyacinthoides non-scripta
English bluebell

◗ ◗ Sp 4-9 ⁝ 10-14in · · 4-6in

Tuft forming bulb. Bright green,
upright leaves. Erect flower stem,
arched at tip, with fragrant, tube-like,
blue bells, the ends of which curl
back at the mouth.

Hyacinthus orientalis
Hyacinth

○ ◇ Sp 5-9 ⁝ 8-12in · · 3-4in

Clump forming bulb. Semi-erect, wide,
glossy leaves. Lax flowering spike with
small, waxy, bell-shaped, very fragrant,
pale blue flowers with recurved tips.

Iris flavescens 'Florentina' Orris

○ ◇ Sp 5-9 ⁝ 3ft · · indefinite

Spring flowering, bearded, intermittent
iris with pale blue-white flowers the

throats of which are delicate yellow.
The leaves are sword-shaped, arching,
and narrow. Alternative I. x germanica
var. florentina

Iris pallida Dalmatian iris

○ ◇ Sp 5-9 ⁝ 28-36in · · indefinite

Rhizomatous iris. Large, lilac-blue,
scented flowers with yellow beards, in
late spring and early summer. Long,
arching, lance-shaped leaves.

Lilium candidum Madonna lily

○ ◇ >7 Su 6-9 ⁝ 3-6ft · · 8-10in

Stiff flowering stem with narrow leaves,
outward-facing, pure white, fragrant,
trumpet-shaped flowers flaring widely
at the mouth.

Lilium 'Connecticut King'

○ ◇ Su 3-8 ⁝ 3ft · · 8-10in

A hybrid with upward-facing, cup-
shaped, bright yellow flowers
contrasting with narrow green leaves
also borne on the upright stem.

Lilium monadelphum

○ ◇ Su 5-8 ⁝ 3-5ft · · 8-10in

Stem has scattered, lance-shaped leaves
and, at the top, nodding, scented,
turkscap flowers, yellow with purple
or deep red spots on the side.

Lilium pumilum

○ ◇ Su 3-8 ⁝ 10-24in · · 6-8in

Stem has small, scattered, linear leaves
and scented, flat, vivid scarlet turkscap
flowers, some black-sspotted in center.

Lilium pyrenaicum
Yellow turkscap lily

○ ◇ Sp 4-7 ⁝ 1-4ft · · 8-10in

Stem has scattered, linear, hairless
leaves and nodding, turkscap flowers
unpleasantly scented. Long petals are
green-yellow to yellow with deep
purple lines and spots. Alternative
L. p. 'Aureum' has yellow flowers

Lilium regale Regal lily

○ ◇ Su 4-7 ⁝ 3-6ft · · 6-8in

Lily with linear leaves and fragrant,
outward-facing, trumpet-shaped
flowers. Long petals, white inside
with yellow base, pink-purple outside
with protruding golden anthers.

Narcissus 'Cheerfulness'

○ ◇ Sp 3-8 ⁝ 16in · · 6in

Fragrant, double white flowers that
have cream and yellow segments in the
center. Very good for cutting.

Narcissus pseudonarcissus
Wild daffodil

○ △ Sp 4-9 ⫶ 6-14in ·· 2-4in
Very variable, early flowering daffodil with fragrant, usually solitary, nodding flower. Overlapping, straw yellow outer petals surround darker yellow trumpet flared at the mouth.

Narcissus 'Tête-à-Tête'
Daffodil

○ △ Sp 3-8 ⫶ 6-8in ·· 2in
Dwarf, early flowering bulb. Long-lasting flowers with reflexed, rich, golden-yellow petals, warm orange-yellow hexagonal trumpet. Arching leaves.

Nerine bowdenii 'Wellsii'
Guernsey lily

○ △ F 8-10 ⫶ 18-24in ·· 3-4in
Strap-shaped, semi-erect basal leaves. Pink flowers with recurved tips. Needs a warm wall.

Orchis mascula
Early purple orchid

○ △ Sp 5-7 ⫶ 8-16in ·· 8in
Terrestrial, deciduous orchid. Shiny, oblong, dark green leaves, often with purple blotches. Bright purple-crimson, helmet-shaped flowers with drooping lip. Unpleasant smell. Alternative *Dactylorhiza fuchsii*

Tulipa humilis

○ △ Sp 5-9 ⫶ 8in ·· 3-4in
Early flowering species. Gray-green, slightly arching leaves, magenta-pink flowers with yellow center.

Tulipa linifolia
Batalini Group 'Red Gem'

○ △ Sp 3-8 ⫶ 4-6in ·· 4in
Early flowering hybrid. Gray-green leaves, orange-red flowers with purple-black centers.

Tulipa saxatilis Cretan tulip

○ △ Sp 3-8 ⫶ 4-6in ·· 14in
Early flowering species. Slightly arching, narrow, shiny green leaves. Scented, mid pink flowers yellow at the base. Needs very warm, sunny spot.

Tulipa turkestanica

○ △ Sp 3-8 ⫶ 4-12in ·· 4in
Early flowering species. Gray-green leaves, hairy, flowering stem. Flowers, with unpleasant odor, have oval, white petals flushed green or pink outside, orange-yellow in the center.

Vanda dearei Orchid

◗ △ Su 10-11 ⫶ 18in ·· 12in
Epiphytic orchid. Flat, oblong, dull green leaves. Large, flat flowers, lemon-yellow or cream, brown veined and scented. *V. tricolor* has pink flowers. Alternative *V. coerulea*

Flowering Annuals and Perennials

Agrostemma githago
Corncockle

○ △ Su 6-9 ⫶ 2-3ft ·· 12in
Erect annual with lance-shaped, mid green leaves, open, trumpet-shaped, pink flowers. Grows best in poor soil. Seeds are poisonous.
Alternative *A. g.* 'Milas'

Anemone x hybrida
Japanese anemone

○ △ Su 4-8 ⫶ 4-5ft ·· 2-4ft
Vigorous, upright perennial. Deeply divided, dark green leaves, cup-shaped single flowers, white to bright pink, late summer to the fall. Can be invasive.

Anthurium andraeanum
Tail flower

◗ ◗ Su 10-11 ⫶ 24-30in ·· 20in
Evergreen, erect perennial. Oval, leathery, long-stalked, dark green leaves. The flower is surrounded by heart-shaped, bright red, long-lasting spathes.

Aquilegia canadensis
Canadian columbine

○ △ Su 7-8 ⫶ 2-3ft ·· 12-14in
Clump forming, leafy perennial with dark green, fern-like foliage. In early summer, slender flowering stem bears bell-shaped, semi-pendent, lemon-yellow flowers with red spurs.

Aubrieta 'Purple Cascade'

○ △ Sp 5-7 ⫶ 4in ·· 8in
Trailing annual. Small, soft green leaves almost obscured by masses of purple-blue flowers in spring and summer.

Bellis perennis
English Daisy

○ △ Sp 4-8 ⫶ 4in ·· 4in
Carpeting perennial with oval, mid green leaves. White, daisy flower in early spring. Often grows in lawns.

Campanula latiloba Bellflower

○ △ Su 4-8 ⫶ 3ft ·· 18in
Wiry flowering stem rises from a rosette of oval leaves bearing shallow, widely cup-shaped flowers in shades of blue, occasionally white or mauve-pink.

Convallaria majalis
Lily-of-the-valley

◗ ◗ Sp 2-7 ⫶ 8-12in ·· 12-16in
Deciduous, rhizomatous, low growing perennial with narrowly oval, mid to dark green leaves. In late spring, pendulous, fragrant, white, bell-shaped flowers between pairs of leaves.

Convolvulus tricolor

○ △ Su 9-10 ⫶ 8-12in ·· 8in
Fast growing, bushy, upright annual with mid green, oval to lance-shaped leaves. Trumpet- to saucer-shaped, blue and white flowers with a yellow-white center. Alternative *C. t.* 'Ensign Hybrids.'

Delphinium elatum hybrids

○ △ Su 3-7 ⫶ 4½-7ft ·· ½-3ft
Erect perennial. Large, palmate leaves with tall flowering spire of densely packed, individual flowers in a range of colors. 'Blue Nile', rich blue flowers streaked light blue, white eyes. 'Butterball', creamy eyed, white flowers. 'Mighty Atom', mid violet, yellow brown or violet marked eyes.

Dianthus 'Haytor White' Pink

○ △ Su 4-8 ⫶ 12in ·· 10-16in
Evergreen, clump forming perennial. Silver-gray, narrow leaves. In mid-summer, masses of double, pure white, fragrant flowers with fringed petals.

Dianthus gratianopolitanus
Cheddar Pink

○ △ Su 3-8 ⫶ 4-10in ·· 10-16in
Evergreen perennial that produces a mat of gray-green, narrow leaves. In mid-summer, the slender stems carry very fragrant, single, pink flowers with a wavy fringe. Perfect plant for a rock garden.

Dianthus 'Musgrave's Pink'

○ △ Su 4-8 ⫶ 10-18in ·· 10-14in
One of the earliest hybrid pinks, dating from c.1730. Narrow, gray-green leaves and scented, single white flowers with a green eye and a frilly edge, in mid-summer. Alternative *D.* 'Telstar Hybrids'

Dictamnus albus Burning bush

○ △ Su 3-8 ⫶ 18-36in ·· 18-24in
Upright perennial. Light green leaves divided into oval leaflets smelling of lemon when crushed. In summer, fragrant, white, star-shaped flowers with long stamens followed by star-shaped seed pods. *D. a.* var. *purpureus* has pink flowers.

Digitalis x mertonensis
Foxglove

◗ ◗ Sp 3-8 ⫶ 30in ·· 30in
Perennial with rosette of soft, hairy, oval leaves. Tall spires of tubular, downward pointing flowers, bruised pink to copper-mauve in summer.

Epimedium x versicolor
'Neosulphureum'

◗ △ Sp 5-9 ⫶ 10-30in ·· 12-16in
Dense, carpeting perennial. Heart-shaped leaves tinted reddish purple in spring; fine fall color. Clusters of small, pale yellow, cup-shaped flowers. Alternative *E. x v.* 'Sulphureum'

Erysimum cheiri Wallflower

○ △ Sp 6-7 ⫶ 10-30in ·· 12-16in
Evergreen, bushy perennial usually grown as biennial. Short, lance-shaped, mid to deep green leaves. Heads of sweetly fragrant flowers, mainly orange and yellow, but they range from deep velvety red to white.

Geranium renardii

○ △ Su 6-8 ⫶ 12in ·· 12in
Compact, clump forming perennial. Sage-green, circular, lobed, velvety leaves. Flat white flowers, sometimes with purple veining, in early summer.

Geranium sanguineum
Bloody cranesbill

○ △ Su 4-8 ⫶ 8-12in ·· 8-12in
Spreading, clump forming perennial. Dark green, finely-cut leaves. In summer, covered with masses of bright magenta-pink, cup-shaped flowers with white eyes.

Geranium sylvaticum
'Mayflower' Wood cranesbill

◗ △ Su 4-8 ⫶ 3ft ·· 2ft
Upright, clump forming perennial with deeply lobed, soft, bright green, slightly aromatic leaves. Branching stems of cup-shaped, violet-blue, white-eyed flowers in early summer.

Gypsophila paniculata
'Bristol Fairy' Baby's breath
○ △ Su 4-9 ⦂ 24-30in · · 3ft
Perennial with wiry, branching stems and masses of tiny, white, double flowers in summer. The leaves are small and dark green.

Hedychium coronarium
Butterfly lily
○ ◗ Su 9-10 ⦂ 6ft · · 2-3ft
Upright perennial. Lance-shaped, green leaves that are downy beneath. The pyramidal flowering spike is densely packed with white, fragrant, butterfly-like flowers, which have yellow blotches near the base.

Hemerocallis lilioasphodelus
Daylily
○ ◗ Sp 3-9 ⦂ 30-36in · · 30-36 in
Spreading, clump forming perennial. Narrow, sword-shaped, mid green leaves. Delicate, upright flowering spike with large, very fragrant, trumpet-shaped, lemon-yellow flowers in late spring and early summer.

Hemerocallis **'Stafford'**
○ ◗ Su 3-9 ⦂ 30in · · 24in
Clump forming, vigorous perennial with strap-shaped, mid green leaves. Bright red, large, trumpet-shaped flowers have maroon and yellow throats with a yellow mid-rib on each of the petals.

Hesperis matronalis
Dame's violet/Sweet rocket
○ △ Su 4-9 ⦂ 30in · · 24in
Upright biennial or short-lived perennial. Smooth, narrowly oval leaves. Long, upright spikes of densely clustered, small, violet or white flowers give off a strong fragrance on warm summer evenings.

Inula helenium Elecampane
○ △ Su 5-8 ⦂ 10ft · · 24in
Robust perennial with a thick, aromatic rhizome. Stout, branching, erect stem with tapering leaves up to 30in in length. Produces a mass of daisy-like, bright yellow flowers.

Inula hookeri
○ △ Su 4-8 ⦂ 30in · · 18in
Clump forming, upright perennial. Hairy, lance-shaped, bright green leaves. Masses of large, daisy-like, slightly scented, yellowish-green flowers with orange center. Alternative *I. orientalis*

Iris, bearded
○ △ Su 4-9 ⦂ varies · · indefinite
Rhizomatous spreading perennial. The group covers the majority of irises, distinct because the large flowers have "beards" of numerous, often colored hairs along the center of the drooping petals ("fall"). 'Carnaby' (⦂ 3ft), in early summer, pale pink flowers with deep, rose-pink fall, orange beards. 'Early Light' (⦂ 3ft), cream-lemon fall, yellow beard. 'Flamenco' (⦂ 3ft), gold-infused beard with red, white to yellow fall. 'Stepping Out' (⦂ 3ft), fall and beard deep purple with blue marks.

Kniphofia **'Erecta'** Torch lily
○ △ Su 6-9 ⦂ 20-60in · · 24-30in
Evergreen perennial. Coarse edged, upright, arching, narrow lance-shaped, blue-green leaves. Stout stem bears terminal spike of densely clustered red, upward-pointing florets in late summer, early fall.

Lewisia rediviva Bitter root
○ △ <7 Sp 5-8 ⦂ ½-1½in · · 2in
Tufted, rosetted perennial. Large pink (or white) many-petalled flowers, late spring to early summer. Small, narrow leaves hidden by flowers in summer.

Lupinus perennis Wild lupine
○ △ >7 Sp 4-9 ⦂ 24in · · 18in
Perennial. Leaves with eight narrow leaflets. Spikes of small blue (rarely pink or white flowers), from late spring to early summer.

Lychnis chalcedonica
Maltese cross
○ △ Su 4-8 ⦂ 3-4ft · · 12-18in
Neat, clump forming perennial. Mid green, slightly hairy leaves. Domed head of small, scarlet flowers with notched petals contrasting with foliage.

Lychnis flos-jovis
Flower of Jove
○ △ Su 4-8 ⦂ 18in · · 18in
Clump forming perennial. Narrow, pointed, silver-gray foliage. Rounded clusters of deep purplish-pink flowers with notched petals.

Matthiola incana Gillyflower
○ △ Su 4-8 ⦂ 12-24in · · 12in
Upright, bushy, fast growing, short lived perennial usually grown as annual. Grayish-green leaves, light purple flowers.

Meconopsis betonicifolia
Himalayan blue poppy
● ◗ <7 Sp 6-8 ⦂ 3-4ft · · 18in
Clump forming perennial. Hairs give a slight rusty tint to basal and stem leaves. In late spring, early summer, papery, bright purplish-blue flowers.

Myosotis sylvatica
Wood forget-me-not
○ △ Sp 5-9 ⦂ 18in · · 18in
Perennial, usually grown as biennial. Dark green leaves with bristle-like hairs, clusters of small, pale blue (rarely white) flowers, late spring and summer.

Oenothera biennis
Evening primrose
○ △ Su 4-8 ⦂ 3-4ft · · 12-18in
Upright biennial with oval, toothed leaves. Cup-shaped, primrose-yellow, silky flowers, sometimes fragrant, open in the evening. May become invasive.

Osteospermum **'Whirligig'**
Sailor daisy
○ △ Su 10-11 ⦂ 24in · · 12-18in
Evergreen, clump forming, prostrate perennial. Profusion of single white flowers with collar of florets like mini spoons. Leaves are gray-green.

Pachystachys lutea
Golden candles
◗ △ Su 10-11 ⦂ 4ft · · 3ft
Evergreen, shrubby perennial with ovate, heavily veined leaves. Tall flower spike is four-sided due to arrangement of yellow gold, large oval bracts.

Paeonia lactiflora
'White Wings' Peony
○ △ Su 3-8 ⦂ 32in · · 24-48in
Clump forming perennial with glossy, dark green leaves that color in the fall. Masses of large, single, fragrant white flowers with slightly ruffled petals, on red flower stalks.

Papaver rhoeas Field poppy
○ △ Su 3-7 ⦂ 24in · · 12in
Fast growing annual with basal rosette of finely cut leaves. Single, delicate, paper-like, cup-shaped scarlet flowers.

Papaver somniferum
Opium poppy
○ △ Su 3-8 ⦂ 18-36in · · 24-36in
Upright, fast growing annual. Light grayish-green, oblong leaves. Large single double flowers with papery petals, red, pink, purple, or white.

Pilosella aurantiaca
Fox-and-cubs/
Orange hawkweed
○ △ Su 5-9 ⦂ 12-18in · · 12in
Mound forming, invasive perennial. Upright, slightly arching, oval, downy leaves. Dandelion-like orange-brown flowers on wiry stems.

Polygonatum odoratum
Fragrant Solomon's seal
● △ Sp 4 8 ⦂ 24in · · 12 18in
Rhizomatous, arching perennial. Green leaflets, tubular to bell-shaped, fragrant, green-tipped white flowers hang from the underside of the leaves. *P. x hybridum*, hybrid of *P. o.* and *P. multiflorum*, has ivory flowers.

Primula florindae
Giant cowslip
○ ◗ Su 3-8 ⦂ 24-36in · · 24-36in
Upright, bold, clump forming perennial. Tall stems crowned with ring of numerous lemon to sulfur yellow flowers in early to mid-summer.

Primula veris Cowslip
○ ◗ Sp 5-8 ⦂ 6-8in · · 6-8in
Clump forming perennial with oval to lance-shaped, mid green, toothed leaves. Clusters of fragrant, yellow, tubular flowers on a stout stem.

Primula vialii
○ ◗ Su 6-7 ⦂ 6-18in · · 9-12in
Short-lived, clump forming perennial. Rosette of upright, hairy leaves. Dense conical spike with mauve florets open from scarlet calyces in late spring.

Primula vulgaris Primrose
○ ◗ Sp 5-8 ⦂ 6-18in · · 10-14in
Neat, clump forming perennial. Rosette of bright green, toothed leaves. Clusters of soft yellow flowers in early spring.

Pulsatilla vulgaris
Pasque flower
○ △ Sp 4-9 ⦂ 6-9in · · 6-9in
Nodding, cup-shaped, lilac or white flowers with golden anthers above the ferny tufts of feathery, soft, hairy leaves, followed by feathery seed heads.

Silene dioica Red campion
○ △ Sp 4-8 ⦂ 12-18in · · 9-12in
Rather leggy and untidy biennial or perennial. Upright, arching stems, oval, green leaves. Clusters of bright pink flowers. *S. d. alba* has white flowers. Alternative *S. uniflora*

Stokesia laevis Stokes' aster

○ △ Su 5-9 ↕ 12-18in ↔ 12-18in
Perennial with over-wintering rosette of leaves. White cornflower-like flowers on the tops of stems. Pointed leaves with white mid vein.

Thermopsis villosa
Carolina lupin

○ △ Su 6-8 ↕ 3ft ↔ 24in
A straggling perennial with glaucous leaves divided into three oval leaflets. In late summer, long stems have racemes of yellow, pea-like flowers.

Trillium grandiflorum
White wake robin/Trillium

● ◗ Sp 4-9 ↕ 18in-24in ↔ 18in-24in
Clump forming perennial. Large, pure white, triangular-shaped flowers with yellow centers above a mound of dark green, arrow-shaped leaves.

Veronica chamaedrys
Germander speedwell

○ △ Su 3-8 ↕ 10in ↔ 8in
Rhizomatous perennial. Upright, branching stems. Gray-green leaves are oval and slightly hairy. Short flowering spike bearing small blue flowers with white throat in late spring and summer.

Veronica spicata
Spiked speedwell

○ △ Su 4-9 ↕ 24-32in ↔ 6-12in
Clump forming perennial. Narrow, oval, toothed, mid green leaves. Small flowering stems produce spikes of small, star-shaped, bright blue flowers. The whole plant is covered with small, silver hairs.

Vicia cracca Tufted vetch

○ △ Sp 5-8 ↕ 12-36in ↔ 12in
Small, oblong leaflets with terminal tendril. Flowers, small, pea-like, deep purple, borne along a flowering stalk.

Viola cornuta 'Alba'
White horned violet

○ △ Su 7-9 ↕ 5-8in ↔ 8in
Rhizomatous perennial. Toothed, oval, bright green leaves. Early to late summer, erect flower stalks with white, angular, flat-faced, spurred flowers.

Viola odorata English violet

○ △ Wi/Sp 5-8 ↕ 4-6in ↔ 12-18in
Semi-evergreen, spreading perennial. Toothed, heart-shaped leaves. Flat-faced, sweetly scented, blue or white flower, sometimes in late winter.

Viola tricolor Heartsease

○ △ Sp 4-8 ↕ 2-6in ↔ 2-6in
Short lived perennial often grown as an annual. Short, arrow-shaped leaves, flat-faced flowers in combinations of yellow, white, and shades of purple. Will go on flowering until the fall.

Flowering Shrubs

Abelia x grandiflora

○ △ Su 6-9 ↕ 10ft ↔ 10ft
Vigorous, branched, medium-sized, semi-evergreen shrub. Dark, glossy green foliage, arching habit. Masses of scented, star-shaped, pink-tinged, white flowers from mid-summer to the fall.

Allamanda 'Golden Sprite'

○ △ Su 10-11 ↕ 3ft ↔ 3ft
Small, compact shrub with glossy, leathery, light green, evergreen foliage. Small, brilliant yellow flowers, chocolate brown in bud, all year round.

Artemisia arborescens Mugwort

○ △ Su 5-8 ↕ 5ft ↔ 5ft
Upright, evergreen shrub. Soft, silver-white, finely cut, aromatic foliage. Small, gray-green flowers with yellow-brown centers, late summer to fall.

Buddleja davidii 'Black Knight'
Butterfly bush

○ △ Su 6-9 ↕ 8-12ft ↔ 8-12ft
Deciduous, vigorous, arching shrub. Long, deep green, lance-shaped leaves, white felted beneath. Plumes of tiny, tubular, dark violet-purple flowers from mid-summer until fall.

Camellia japonica 'Tricolor'

◗ △ <7 Sp 7-8 ↕ 10-20ft ↔ 3-10ft
Compact evergreen shrub. Glossy, dark green, oval leaves. This cultivar has semi-double, medium-sized flowers, white streaked with rich crimson.

Camellia sasanqua

◗ △ <7 F 7-8 ↕ 10-20ft ↔ 10-15ft
Dense, upright, fast growing evergreen shrub. Long, oval-shaped, bright green leaves. This species is a little unusual, bearing many flattish to cup-shaped, single, fragrant, white flowers in fall.

Camellia x williamsii
'Donation'

◗ △ <7 Sp 7-9 ↕ 6-15ft ↔ 3-10ft
Evergreen, upright, spreading shrub with small, glossy, mid green leaves. In

spring, the bush bears a mass of semi-double, cup-shaped, pink flowers.

Carpenteria californica
Tree anemone

○ ◗ Su 9-10 ↕ 6ft ↔ 6ft
Evergreen, domed, bushy shrub. Lance-shaped, dark green, glossy leaves and white, fragrant, yellow-centered, camellia-like flowers all summer long.

Chimonanthus praecox
Wintersweet

○ △ Wi 7-9 ↕ 8ft ↔ 10ft
Bushy, deciduous shrub. In winter, bare branches covered with stalkless, almost translucent-yellow, scented flowers. Roughly oval, glossy, dark green leaves.

Cistus salviifolius Rock rose

○ △ Su 7-9 ↕ 30in ↔ 30in
Dense, bushy, evergreen shrub. Gray-green, wrinkled foliage forming a dome. Masses of white, cup-shaped flowers with central yellow blotches throughout early summer.

Cistus x cyprius

○ △ Su 7-9 ↕ 5ft ↔ 5ft
Bushy, evergreen shrub with glossy, dark green, narrow, sticky leaves. Large, white flowers with a yellow center and red blotch at the base of each petal are borne in early summer.

Correa 'Mannii'
Australian fuchsia

○ △ Su 9-10 ↕ 6ft ↔ 6ft
Bushy, slender-stemmed, evergreen shrub. Oval, narrow leaves, slightly hairy beneath. Tubular, scarlet, pendent flowers appear intermittently from late summer to spring.

Daphne mezereum Mezereon

○ △ Wi 5-8 ↕ 4ft ↔ 3-4ft
Upright, deciduous shrub. Fragrant, small, pink or purple flowers smother bare stems in winter, followed by red fleshy berries, dull, gray-green leaves.

Daphne odora 'Aureomarginata'

○ △ Wi/Sp 7-9 ↕ 5-6ft ↔ 5-6ft
Bushy, evergreen shrub with dark green, oval leaves narrowly edged with yellow. From mid-winter to early spring, tight clusters of fragrant, starry flowers appear at the tips of the stems.

Daphne x burkwoodii 'Astrid'

○ △ Sp 5-8 ↕ 5ft ↔ 5ft
Upright, bushy, semi-evergreen shrub. Clusters of fragrant, white and pink

flowers in spring, occasionally second flowering in the fall. Mid green, lance-shaped leaves edged with creamy white.

Euonymus europaeus
European euonymus

○ △ F 5-7 ↕ 6-10ft ↔ 6-10ft
Bushy, deciduous shrub. Mid green, narrow, oval leaves turn red in the fall. Grown for the spectacular purplish-pink fruit borne in the fall, which split to reveal orange seed coats.

Fothergilla major
Large fothergilla

◗ ◗ <7 Sp 5-8 ↕ 6-8ft ↔ 4-6ft
Deciduous, upright shrub. Fragrant, bottle-brush tufts of white flowers on bare stems in spring. Glossy, dark green, oval leaves turn scarlet and orange in the fall.

Grevillea rosmarinifolia

○ △ <7 Su 9-10 ↕ 6ft ↔ 6ft
Rounded, well branched, evergreen shrub. Dense clusters of tubular, red flowers. Dark green leaves, silky haired beneath, shaped like those of rosemary.

Halimium 'Susan'

○ △ Su 9-10 ↕ 18in ↔ 24cm
Small, spreading, evergreen shrub. Dark green, fairly small, oval leaves. Bright yellow, cup-shaped flowers with prominent filament like yellow anthers. May become invasive.

Hamamelis mollis Witch hazel

○ △ Wi 5-8 ↕ 12ft ↔ 12ft
Deciduous, open, upright shrub. In winter, fragrant yellow, spider-like flowers on bare branches. Oval, mid green leaves turn red, orange, and yellow in the fall.

Heliotropium arborescens
Heliotrope

○ △ Sp 10-11 ↕ 30in ↔ 3ft
Bushy, evergreen, short-lived shrub. Finely wrinkled, semi-glossy, dark green leaves. Flat clusters of slightly scented purple to white flowers from late spring until winter. Often grown as an annual.

Hypericum androsaemum
Tutsan

◗ △ Su 7-8 ↕ 30in ↔ 30in
Deciduous shrub with oval, rich green leaves. Small, star-shaped, yellow flowers, followed by round black berries in the fall.

Kalmia latifolia
Mountain laurel

○ ▶ <7 Su 4-9 ⁝ 10ft · · 10ft

Evergreen, bushy, dense shrub. Leathery, dark green leaves, almost obscured by large clusters of pink, bowl-shaped flowers.

Mahonia aquifolium 'Apollo'
Oregon grape

▶ ▶ Sp 6-9 ⁝ 2ft · · 5ft

Evergreen, open shrub. Leaves of bright green, glossy leaflets often turn purple and red in winter. Large clusters of bright yellow flowers, followed by grape-like blue-black berries.

Philadelphus x temoisei 'Erectus' Mock orange

○ △ Su 5-8 ⁝ 4-10ft · · 14-10ft

Deciduous, open branched shrub. Oval, dark green leaves, masses of fragrant white flowers.

Potentilla fruticosa 'Red Ace'

▶ △ Sp 3-7 ⁝ 30in · · 5ft

Spreading, dense, bushy, deciduous shrub. Narrow, compact, lance-shaped, gray-green to dark green leaves. Bright vermilion flowers with yellow centers, from late spring to mid fall.

Rhododendron 'Elizabeth'

▶ △ <7 Sp 7-9 ⁝ 3ft · · 3ft

Evergreen, dome-shaped shrub. Oblong leaves and trusses of large, brilliant red, trumpet-shaped flowers.

Rhododendron falconeri

▶ ▶ <7 Sp 8-9 ⁝ 25-40ft · · 10-20ft

Evergreen, upright, large shrub with cinnamon-colored bark, long, deep green, leathery leaves with yellowy veins, orange beneath. Large trusses of creamy yellow, bell-shaped flowers marked purple inside.

Rhododendron luteum Azalea

▶ ▶ <7 Sp 6-9 ⁝ 8-12ft · · 7-10ft

Deciduous shrub with open habit. Masses of funnel-shaped, bright yellow, richly fragrant flowers. Oblong, lance-shaped leaves color richly in the fall.

Rosa 'Aloha'

○ △ Su 5-9 ⁝ 8ft · · 8ft

Stiff, bushy, climbing rose. Leaves leathery, dark green. Large, cup-shaped, fully double, fragrant rose- and salmon-pink flowers, late summer and fall.

Rosa x damascena
Damask rose

○ △ Su 4-9 ⁝ 6ft · · 5ft

Small shrub with grayish-green leaves. Large, fragrant flowers, red to white, followed by white hips. *R. d.* var. *versicolor*, unusual form with loose, double, white flowers with irregular flakes of pink or rose-red blotches.

Rosa gallica var. officinalis
Apothecary's rose

○ △ 4-9 ⁝ 3ft · · 3ft

Old, well-loved rose. Neat, bushy habit, dark green leaflets. Masses of richly fragrant, semi-double, rosy crimson flowers with prominent yellow anthers.

Rosa hemisphaerica
Sulfur rose

○ △ Su 4-9 ⁝ 6ft · · 4ft

Medium-sized shrub with sea-green leaflets. Sweetly scented, double, sulfur yellow flowers throughout the summer.

Rosa 'Madame Hardy'

○ △ Su 4-9 ⁝ 5ft · · 4ft

Vigorous, upright, damask rose. Leathery, matte green leaves. Richly scented, fully double white flowers with green centers.

Rosa moschata Musk rose

○ △ Su 7-9 ⁝ 6-12ft · · 10ft

Vigorous, somewhat lax shrub. Glossy, dark green leaflets. Late summer to fall, large flowerheads with musk scented, cream white flowers.

Rosa rubiginosa Sweet briar

○ △ Su 4-9 ⁝ 8ft · · 8ft

Vigorous, arching thorny branches with apple scented foliage. Clear pink flowers in summer. Oval hips turn bright red in the fall.

Rosa virginiana

○ △ Su 3-9 ⁝ 3ft · · 5ft

Small, suckering shrub. Glossy green leaves turn purple, then crimson and yellow in the fall. Bright pink flowers.

Telopea speciosissima
Waratah

○ △ >7 Su 10-11 ⁝ 10ft · · 6ft

Bushy, erect evergreen shrub. Coarse, serrated, oval leaves. Large showy flowerhead has bright red, petal-like bracts surrounding the small, tubular red flowers.

Viburnum carlesii
Korean spice viburnum

○ △ Sp 5-7 ⁝ 5-6ft · · 6ft

Rounded, deciduous, bushy shrub with dark green leaves that turn red in the fall. Pink buds open to scented, white-and-pink flowers. Black fruit.

Viburnum tinus Laurustinus

○ △ Wi/Sp 8-10 ⁝ 8-12ft · · 10ft

Dense, evergreen, bushy shrub. Oval, dark green leaves. Flat heads of small white flowers from late winter through spring, followed by blue-black fruit.

Viburnum x bodnantense 'Dawn'

○ △ Wi/Sp 7-8 ⁝ 8-12ft · · 5-8ft

Upright, deciduous shrub. Oval leaves bronze at first, later bright green. Clusters of deep pink buds open to very fragrant, pink flowers, from late fall to early spring.

Water Plants and Marginals

Carex elata 'Aurea'
Bowles' golden sedge

○ ▲ 5-9 ⁝ 20-28in · · 16-20in

Tuft forming, evergreen perennial sedge. Narrow, upright, arching, bright yellow leaves with narrow borders. Brown-black flower spikes in summer.

Iris pseudacorus Yellow flag

● ▲ Su 5-8 ⁝ 3-5ft · · 12-18in

Vigorous beardless iris. Broad, ridged, grayish-green, sword-like leaves. Branched stem with yellow-gold flowers, often brown or violet veining.

Matteuccia struthiopteris
Ostrich fern

▶ ▲ 3-8 ⁝ 3-5ft · · 24-36in

Deciduous, rhizomatous fern with outer rim of gently arching, yellow-green fronds, inside which are shorter greenish brown fronds. Both sets spear-shaped, very thin, and deeply cut with blackish-brown mid-ribs.

Nymphaea 'American Star'
Water lily

○ Su 4-11 · · 4ft

Deciduous perennial with heart-shaped, floating leaves, purple-bronze when young, later bright green. In summer, deep pink, star-shaped, semi-double flowers are held above the water.

Nymphaea nouchali var. caerulea Blue water lily

○ Su 10-11 · · 4ft

Bright green, heart-shaped leaves, and many-petalled flowers. Each petal is light blue at the tip, shading to purple at the base. The center of the flower is deep yellow.

Nymphaea 'Marliacea Albida'
Water lily

○ Su 4-11 · · 6ft

Deciduous perennial with deep green, heart-shaped leaves with purple-green undersides. Pure white, cup-shaped, semi-double, fragrant flowers are produced in summer.

Osmunda regalis
Royal fern

▶ ● 4-9 ⁝ 6ft · · 3ft

Deciduous fern with broadly triangular, divided, bright green fronds, pinkish when young. Mature plants have rust-brown, tassel-like flower spikes at the ends of taller fronds.

index

Page numbers in *italics* refer to illustrations

INNISFIL PUBLIC LIBRARY

acknowledgments

Key: p = page, t = top, c = center, b = bottom, l = left, r = right, GPL = Garden Picture Library, des = designer

Front and back endpapers Jerry Harpur/des: Thomas Church, **p1** GPL/Lamontagne, **p2** GPL/Gary Rogers, **p3** Melanie Eclare, **p4/5** GPL/Steven Wooster, **p6/7** Tim Street-Porter/Galuez/Baragán, **p8** Jerry Harpur/des: Tom Hobbs, **p9** t GPL/Gary Rogers, c Hugh Palmer/Polly Park, b GPL/Ron Sutherland, **p10** Jerry Harpur/Jean-Pierre Chalon, **p11** GPL/Steven Wooster, **p12/13** Jerry Harpur/des: Penelope Hobhouse, **p13** r Steven Wooster, **p14/15** GPL/Michael Paul, **p16** Jerry Harpur/Crowinshield, USA, **p17** t Bridgeman Art Library/Waterhouse and Dodd, London, b Jerry Harpur/Crowinshield, USA, **p18** t GPL/Gary Rogers, b Jerry Harpur/des: Christopher Masson, London, **p20** t Bridgeman Art Library/Victoria and Albert Museum, London, c GPL/Marijke Heuff, b Jerry Harpur/Daniel Baneuil, **p21** Hugh Palmer/Casa de Pilatos, **p23** The Interior Archive/Simon Upton/des:Grazia Gazzoni, **p24** Bridgeman Art Library/Osterreichische Nationalbibliothek, Vienna, **p25** Melanie Eclare/Les Jardins du Prieuré Notre Dame d'Orsan, France, **p26** Hugh Palmer/ Les Jardins du Prieuré Notre Dame d'Orsan, France, **p28** Jerry Harpur/Ilford Manor, **p29** t Hugh Palmer/Isola Bella, Italy, **p29** b Marcus Harpur/Barnard's, Essex, **p30** The National Trust Picture Library, **p32** t Bridgeman Art Library/Chester Beatty Library and Gallery of Oriental Art, Dublin, b GPL/Michael Paul, **p33** GPL/Steven Wooster, **p34** t GPL/Michael Paul, bl GPL/Michael Paul, br GPL/Ron Sutherland, **p36** GPL/Gary Rogers, **p37** t GPL/Steven Wooster, b Bridgeman Art Library/Museum of the City of New York, **p38** l GPL/Steven Wooster, tr GPL/Gary Rogers, br GPL/Gary Rogers, **p40** l GPL/Brigitte Thomas, r Bridgeman Art Library/Mallet and Son Antiques Ltd, London, **p41** Hugh Palmer/Jenkyn Place, **p42** t GPL/Brigitte Thomas, b Hugh Palmer/Trewithin, **p44/45** Tim Street-Porter/Gilardi, **p45** tr Bridgeman Art Library/tr Bridgeman Art Library/© Fernando Botero, courtesy, Marlborough Gallery, New York, cr GPL/Michael Paul, br The Interior Archive/Cecilia Innes/José Yturbe, **p47** l Tim Street-Porter/Kahlo, tr The Interior Archive/Juan Sordo Madelena, br GPL/Gary Rogers, **p48** l Jerry Harpur/des: Thomas Church, r GPL/Vivian Russell, **p49** Jerry Harpur/des: Thomas Church, **p51** t Jerry Harpur/des: Juan Grimm, b John Brookes Landscape Design/des: John Brookes **p52** Jerry Harpur/des: Topher Delaney, San Francisco, **p53** t Jerry Harpur/des: Topher Delaney, San Francisco b Jerry Harpur/des: Steve Oliver, **p54** l Clive Nichols/des: Christopher Bradley-Hole, r GPL/Steven Wooster, **p56/57** GPL/Gary Rogers, **p58/59** GPL/Gary Rogers, **p59** r GPL/Jerry Pavia, **p60** t GPL/Jerry Pavia, b GPL/Gary Rogers, **p62** GPL/Gary Rogers, **p63** Caroline Jones, **p65** t GPL/Gary Rogers, b Jerry Harpur, **p67** GPL/Steven Wooster, **p69** t GPL/Michael Paul, b GPL/Steven Wooster, **p70** Steven Wooster/Hampton Court Flower Show/des: Bonita Bulaitis, **p71** Melanie Eclare, **p72** t Helen Fickling/des: Diana Yakeley, b Jerry Harpur/des: Tom Hobbs, **p74** t GPL/Ron Sutherland, c Jerry Harpur/Sun House, Long Melford, Suffolk, **p75** Clive Nichols/Sue Berger, **p76** t Hugh Palmer/Tyninghame House, East Linton, Lothian, c Helen Fickling/des: Diana Yakeley, b Helen Fickling/des: Ruth Barclay, **p78/79** GPL/Ron Sutherland, **p81** t Clive Nichols/Simon Irvine, b The Interior Archive/Helen Fickling/des:Catherine Mason, **p82** t GPL/Jerry Pavia, b GPL/Jacqui Hurst, **p84** GPL/Gary Rogers, **p85** Tim Street-Porter/Galuez/Baragán, **p86** t Jerry Harpur, bl GPL/Michael Paul, br GPL/Gary Rogers, **p87** t GPL/Ron Sutherland, b GPL/Gary Rogers, **p90/91** Melanie Eclare/des: Michele Osborne, **p90** l GPL/Ron Sutherland, r GPL/Michael Paul, **p92** l GPL/Steven Wooster/des: Michele Osborne, r GPL/Michael Paul, **p94/95** The Interior Archive/Simon Upton/des: Marja Walters/Michael Reeves, **p96** t Clive Nichols/George Carter/Chelsea '99, b Steven Wooster/The Morrell's Garden, Wainui Beach, NZ, **p97** Arcaid/Garry Sarre/Belle, **p98/99** Jerry Harpur/des: Sonny Garcia, San Francisco, USA, **p98** tl Jerry Harpur/des: Margot Knox, Melbourne, Aus., **p99** r Jerry Harpur/des: Steve Chase, Palm Springs, USA, **p100** t Jerry Harpur/des: Topher Delaney, San Francisco, b GPL/Marijke Heuff, **p101** Clive Nichols/des: Christopher Bradley-Hole, **p102** tl GPL/Michael Paul, bc GPL/Gary Rogers, br Jerry Harpur/des: Stephen Woodhams, **p103** l Clive Nichols/des: Steve Bird, r GPL/John Glover, **p104** Jerry Harpur/des: Robert Watson, **p105** The Interior Archive/Simon Upton/des: Grazia Gazzoni, **p106** Jerry Harpur/Ryoan-ji Temple, Kyoto, **p107** Helen Fickling/des: Ruth Barclay, **p108** cl The InteriorArchive/Herbert Ypma/José Yturbe, bl GPL/Michael Paul, r GPL/John Glover, **p109** t Jerry Harpur, b GPL/Michael Paul, **p110/111** Jerry Harpur/des: Paul Guest, **p110** tl GPL/Steven Wooster, bl GPL/Gil Hanly, **p111** tr Helen Fickling/Anne Birnhak, br GPL/Ron Sutherland, **p112/113** GPL/Steven Wooster, **p112** tl GPL/Marijke Heuff, **p114** Jerry Harpur/Ilford Manor, **p115** Jerry Harpur/des: D Gabouland, **p116** Steven Wooster/Ross & Paula Greenville, **p117** GPL/Ron Sutherland, **p118/119** Jerry Harpur/des: R David Adams, **p118** t Helen Fickling/des: Anne Birnhak, l Helen Fickling/des: Ruth Barclay, **p119** t Jerry Harpur/des: Topher Delaney, San Francisco, **p119** r Jerry Harpur/des: Claude & Andrez Dancel, **p120/121** Clive Nichols/Trevyn McDowell, **p120** t Steven Wooster/des: Michele Osborne, bl Clive Nichols/des: Helen Sinclair & Mike Cedar, **p122/123** The Interior Archive/Fritz von der Schulenburg/des: Nico Rensch, **p124** l Helen Fickling/des: Ruth Barclay, r Helen Fickling/des: Ruth Barclay, **p125** Jerry Harpur/des: Annie Wilkes, **p126** Hugh Palmer, **p127** tl Helen Fickling/des: Diana Yakeley, tr Helen Fickling/des: Ruth Barclay, bl Clive Nichols/Robin Green/Ralph Cade, br Hugh Palmer/Kingstone Cottage, **p128** Terragram Pty Ltd/Walter Glover, **p129** t Andrew Lawson/des: Jane Sweetser, Hampton Court '99, b Terragram Pty Ltd/Walter Glover, **p130** GPL/Gary Rogers, **p131** l GPL/Gary Rogers, r Melanie Eclare/des: Gunilla Pickard, **p132** t Hugh Palmer, b GPL/John Neubauer, **p133** l Helen Fickling/des: Ruth Barclay, tr GPL/Steven Wooster, br Tim Street-Porter/Gilardi, **p134/135** Steven Wooster/James Wright's Garden nr. Aukland, NZ, **p134** l GPL/J.S. Sira, **p136** The Interior Archive/Tim Beddow, **p137** GPL/Garv Rogers, **p138** Hugh Palmer/Pelham Crescent, **p139** t GPL/Michael Paul, b Helen Fickling/des: Diana Yakeley, **p140** l GPL/Brigitte Thomas, tr GPL/Steven Wooster, br GPL/Ron Sutherland, **p141** l Jerry Harpur/Jean Anderson, Seattle, USA, tr Jerry Harpur/des: Thomas Church, br Arcaid/Alan Weintraub, **p142** Helen Fickling/des: Anne Birnhak.

author's acknowledgments

I would like to thank everyone who has worked so hard and unceasingly to make this book a reality, especially Emily Hedges, Casey Horton, Erica Hunningher, Chris Gardner, Fiona Lindsay, Tony Lord, Larraine Shamwana, Jacqui Small, Helen Smythe, Arlene Sobel and Maggie Town. A great thank you is also due to my family and friends who have been so supportive and, of course, to Terry the Cat.

Toby Musgrave's Web site is at www:tobymusgrave.com